BILL MORRIS

GEOFFREY GOODMAN has written for a number of national newspapers including the former *Manchester Guardian*, *News Chronicle*, *Daily Herald*, and *Daily Mirror*. He has also been a foreign correspondent working across Europe, China, the former Soviet Union as well as the United States. He has been a regular broadcaster on BBC radio and television and LBC, and he is founding editor of the *British Journalism Review*. He has won several national press awards including the Gerald Barry Award for Lifetime Achievements in Journalism and in 1998 was appointed CBE for services to journalism.

BILL MORRIS
A Trade Union Miracle

GEOFFREY GOODMAN

Arcadia Books Ltd
15–16 Nassau Street
London W1W 7AB

www.arcadiabooks.com

First published by Arcadia Books 2010

A catalogue record for this book is available from the British Library.

ISBN 978-1-906413-42-2

Typeset in Minion by MacGuru Ltd
Printed and bound in Finland by WS Bookwell

Arcadia Books gratefully acknowledges the financial support of Arts Council England.

Arcadia Books supports PEN, the fellowship of writers who work together to promote
literature and its understanding. English PEN upholds writers' freedoms in Britain and
around the world, challenging political and cultural limits on free expression.
To find out more, visit *www.englishpen.org* or contact
English PEN, 6–8 Amwell Street, London EC1R 1UQ

Arcadia Books distributors are as follows:

in the UK and elsewhere in Europe:
Turnaround Publishers Services
Unit 3, Olympia Trading Estate
Coburg Road
London N22 6TZ

in the USA and Canada:
Independent Publishers Group
814 N. Franklin Street
Chicago, IL 60610

Contents

Introduction

TO BE THE LEADER of any British trade union during the years when that role, indeed even the very existence of trade unions as modern institutions, had come under its most severe challenge for a century was and remains an assignment requiring very special dedication and commitment.

To be the leader of a union that was then not only the largest in the United Kingdom but also an organisation once having the highest membership of any trade union in the non-communist world was a role demanding ability, character and courage well beyond the norm of conventional leadership credentials. Such a person needed the personality, charm and the sagacity of an intellectual magician along with a few additional qualities. Arguably the role has always required these abilities; but in the period of Margaret Thatcher's premiership when she regarded the undermining, if not the destruction, of the trade union ethos as a major priority – to lead a major trade union under those conditions was an entirely enlarged challenge. In effect the objective was to try to re-establish the credibility and *raison d'être* of the institution itself. The man who was elected to fill that role in the Transport and General Workers Union was Bill Morris: William Manuel Morris, now Lord Bill Morris of Handsworth OJ.

It happened that he was black: more to the point he was the first black man to lead a British trade union, in fact the first black man to reach the pinnacle of any major national institution in British history.

Morris came to office as the general secretary of the Transport and General Workers Union after a decade in which Margaret Thatcher's thrice-elected Conservative government had introduced and consolidated legislation which effectively neutralised the role trade unions had played in British political life for most of the twentieth century. Morris's inheritance from his predecessor Ron Todd was a trade union horse weighed down by seemingly impossible new burdens. Yet the newcomer saw all this as an extraordinary challenge rather than an inherited burden. For him, a boy who had been born in a small Jamaican village, it was by any standards an astonishing turn of fate.

So let us, first, consider the nature of the job he was elected to do.

Bill Morris was required to deal, often on a daily (indeed sometimes hourly) basis with government ministers, financiers, bankers, business and industrial leaders across the board; but above all with his own member-ship. That membership at all times would include voices of anger, frustration and certainly personal abuse; all of them voices able to deliver rational, irrational and even cavalier complaints. To be sure they also included voices often skilled in the practice of idle flattery from which the leader of the union, like any other leader, would especially need to be on guard, ever reminded of the warning to all men in authority: be neither sur-prised nor influenced by the menace of cheap praise any more than idle criticism. Both are equally destruc-tive siren voices.

With a membership that embraced over one and half million people covering almost every kind of job in the catalogue of work, it was never the easiest for any trade union official to feel confident of knowing the collective mood of such a diverse membership. Yet that was – and to a large extent remains – the job description and role of the general secretary of the Transport and General Workers Union, the T&G as it was called before it was recently merged to form an even larger combine called UNITE.

This book, however, is about the man who was gen-eral secretary of the TGWU before that merger with another grouping of unions called AMICUS. It is about the man who led the union when it still stood, uniquely, as the single most powerful trade union in Britain – even after Mrs Thatcher's legislative battering. That man is Bill Morris, a unique figure in British life. Not only as the first black person to lead a great British trade union, but equally because his rise to eminence in British life helped to inject a profound sense of fresh confidence throughout the black community. Hardly anybody in that community could ever have envisaged someone from their ranks reaching such a position. It was not considered to be part of their agenda of hope. A dream? Perhaps. But hardly a realistic hope.

However I feel it is important first to explain something about the organisation, the T&G, which enabled a dream to be realised. That trade union is an inextricable part of the story. I would not claim that it could not have been feasible with another trade union, although I do believe it was less likely without the history, political tradition and characteristics of the TGWU. It is in the context of the history of that trade union, in my view, that it became possible for Morris to open new doorways in the continuing, perhaps perpetual, fight against racial discrimination. Which, I daresay, is another way of claiming that this is also the story of an unusual trade union.

This last point raises an important additional factor we need to consider: the general and historic background to the attitude on racial issues within British trade unions. By tradition and history the trade unions in British society have based their philosophy, and a practical agenda of challenging the social and political status quo, on challenging and fighting the class structure and prejudices which have deep roots, and on protesting against the inequalities which inescapably have been inherent within that structure. For the most part, from its earliest beginnings the British trade union movement set a vision for a more equal, humane society with strong socialist undertones as its objective. That ethos was regarded as a foundation stone on which, eventually, the Labour Party itself was created. Yet none of this could conceal the fact that the unions also had to function within a range of social prejudices common to all the classes whether they were from the aristocracy or as, in the case of the trade unions, from a culturally as well as an economically deprived working class. That social climate involved a widespread suspicion of foreigners, white or black. The island race had the not uncommon psychological problem with 'outsiders' of all kinds. It was a characteristic that penetrated across all class boundaries and prevailed strongly even after the end of the Second World War. Disraeli was correct when challenged about his own political allegiance given that much of his behaviour was so unorthodox: 'Ah,' he observed, 'you must remember that the English are a very conservative people.' Substitute 'British' for 'English' and the comment remains entirely relevant.

In that sense the British scene differed from the American experience. The United States was built on welcoming immigrants – preferably white, to be sure. Moreover its discrimination against African-Americans was and remains heavily influenced by the slave trade and therefore contained additional and often quite different elements of prejudice and judgement from attitudes developed by traditional Britons. The British were never enamoured of immigrants since, unlike the early American settlers, they were never persuaded such an investment was an economic necessity. Indeed even in the early post-war years when the first phase of organised immigration began from the West Indies (in the 1950s under a Conservative government), it was regarded as a temporary expedient. Trade unions as well as later Labour governments were slow to recognise that a fundamental shift in the ethnological mix had begun and one that would inevitably change the nature and even the character of British society. Indeed this was one of the major reasons why the views of the late Enoch Powell carried so much controversial influence in the mid-fifties and sixties. Powell's voice, especially by the mid-sixties, had an immediate impact on the white working class, notably among some trade union members, including the Transport and General Workers Union, because he was swift to recognise a cultural change that he regarded as a threat to a broader concept of what it was 'to be British'. Whatever merits or de-merits are associated with the name of Enoch Powell it cannot be denied that he understood the undertones better than many other politicians or even trade union leaders. It is essential to remember these factors when we consider the significance of the rise of Bill Morris.

That is why to explain adequately the role Morris was called on to fill when he became general secretary of the TGWU in 1991, it is important first to set out the nature of the union he came to lead and paint in some of the social and historic background endemic to this remarkable story.

1

The Union That Became a New Home

THE TRANSPORT AND GENERAL WORKERS UNION was an organisation born in 1922 in the aftermath of the First World War when its founder, Ernest Bevin, finally succeeded in bringing together an assorted collection of fourteen smaller unions whose origins went back deep into the nineteenth century. Many of these smaller unions represented isolated trades and crafts that had struggled for years to find a formula which might bring them together in the shape of a larger, stronger, more influential bargaining unit better able to combat the exploitation of working people. These diverse unions covered a range of men (and they were almost entirely male) including road transport workers, dockers, truck drivers, tram and bus drivers and conductors, draymen, warehouse workers, navvies – the semi-skilled and unskilled, all drawn from the developing working classes of the nineteenth and early twentieth century as Britain's industrial power grew. These early trade unions, before the birth of the Labour Party, fought for basic social justice, decency and a civilised voice which they hoped could be heard above the clamour and domination of self-interest and a ruling political class which for most of the nineteenth century had often brutally sidelined voices from what they would describe as 'the lower orders'.

Ernest Bevin, the genius who finally succeeded in bringing together these fourteen separate unions to form the TGWU was fortunate in one sense: he succeeded where others, no doubt equally as talented as Bevin (like Tom Mann), had failed in the days before the First World War. Bevin's timing was the key to his success. He produced his formula to form the T&G in 1921, only a few years after the end of war when hope and idealism were still fresh.

Ernest Bevin was born in the village of Winsford, Somerset, on 7 March 1881. He was an illegitimate child whose name, Bevin, was acquired when his mother married a William Bevin in 1884. Ernest never knew the identity of his biological father, which was not an unusual feature among early leaders of the British Labour Movement. Bevin's first job was in the bakehouse of a Bristol restaurant with a wage of six shillings a week. He then worked as a carter driving a dray, pulled by a horse or horses, loaded with mineral waters. After that came a job as a page boy, followed by a conductor on Bristol's horse-trams ... and so it went on as the boy tasted almost every semi-skilled or more often unskilled job available at the end of the nineteenth century – like most of those jobs connected with the prosperous and developing trades around Bristol's docks, then one of the nation's major trading ports and industrial growth points. It was of course an ideal apprenticeship for the man who was to bring together the smaller unions, most of them involved in the kind of work he himself had been doing before he became a full-time official with the Dockers' Union in 1910. Bevin was then aged twenty-nine.

It was a watershed for Bevin and for British trade unions: the beginning of what was to develop into him becoming Britain's most politically influential trade union leader of all time. And without stretching the point, it was in its own way a foundation stone on which Bill Morris, eighty-one years later, would take his stand as one of Bevin's successors. Similarly, perhaps, to the man from nowhere ...

Once Bevin had formed the T&G in 1922 he then helped to establish the General Council of the Trades Union Congress, the command unit for the entire trade union movement. Throughout the 1920s he continued to play a crucial role as the Labour Party developed, under Ramsay MacDonald's leadership, to become, for the first time, a governing party in Britain – winning the general elections of 1924 and 1929 albeit in both instances without an overall majority. Throughout his premiership both Labour governments under MacDonald operated as minority governments – in government but never, effectively, in power. After the worldwide economic crisis in the early 1930s following the Wall Street collapse of 1929 MacDonald's Labour government split. MacDonald along with several of his former Labour cabinet colleagues went into a national coalition with the Conservative Party forming a national government with the Conservative leader Stanley Baldwin. Bevin was wholly opposed to such an arrangement and he persuaded the trade unions to break with MacDonald and reform the Labour Party in opposition. What followed transformed Bevin from an exceptional trade union leader into a national political figure. Using the T&G as his base Bevin then fought to re-establish the Labour Party as a separate entity and sustain it as a credible political force through to the Second World War. During that war, in which the Labour Party and the Conservatives formed a war coalition under Winston Churchill, one of the Prime Minister's first moves was to invite Ernest Bevin to join his war cabinet as his Minister of Labour – a role in which the leader of the TGWU (who was provided with a Parliamentary seat) was given unprecedented powers to mobilise the nation's manpower resources. In fact it was a role in which Bevin became Churchill's most favoured cabinet colleague. In the meantime with Bevin a government minister, his union (and he did see it as *his* union!) was temporarily under the leadership of one of Bevin's deputies – Arthur Deakin, the assistant general secretary – although Bevin retained a formal entitlement to return to his role as general secretary whenever he wished to do so. In effect Deakin was a 'caretaker leader' of 'Bevin's union', the T&G.

When Labour won the 1945 general election it gained overall power for the first time in its history. The new Prime Minister Clement Attlee appointed Bevin as foreign secretary. At that point Arthur Deakin was finally confirmed as Bevin's successor as general secretary of the T&G. In the early post-war years Deakin himself developed a powerful persona as a national figure in his own right within the trade union world. Yet he never possessed the vision or creative imagination of his predecessor. Deakin's instincts were to preserve a status quo and his principal anxiety was to behave as he assumed Bevin wished – which was a traditional, conservative style of leadership, antipathetic towards most radical and left-wing ideas. Bevin himself in later years, especially after serving in Churchill's war cabinet during the war, abandoned his earlier radical feelings in favour of more moderate centrist policies. The T&G was then seen under Deakin as the standard-bearer for trade union leadership authority regardless of the stirrings of revolt among rank and file membership in most unions.

Then came a series of extraordinary developments which eventually led to a transformation in the direction and policies of the TGWU. Deakin died while in office, and before he could effectively select a preferred successor in his own image. He was succeeded by Arthur 'Jock' Tiffin who would have been ready to turn the union in a more radical direction had he not died within a few months of being elected as Deakin's successor. These two deaths in quick succession combined to leave the largest of Britain's trade unions without a pre-ordained leader; someone who was available after being carefully groomed for the role by his predecessors. It was an astonishing turn of events which led to the election of a leader who had scarcely been heard of outside the trade union community: Frank Cousins, a former miner and truck driver who had risen to become head of the union's road transport section and then, mostly by chance, appointed to the post of deputy general secretary under Tiffin. It was in fact an avalanche of chance and circumstance which was to lead to a completely new phase of political and industrial development not only for the TGWU but also for the whole trade union movement as well as the Labour Party. For Cousins, unlike his predecessors, was a committed man of the radical Left and someone without any inhibitions about overturning accepted policies. This was in almost every sense in complete contrast to Deakin and Bevin. With his election in 1955 Frank Cousins turned the British political scene upside down. And with a touch of pure chance Cousins came to power as head of the union at approximately the time a young black immigrant was arriving in Birmingham. That was a circumstance unknown to both but which was to have a profound influence on the future of the young Bill Morris.

Almost single-handedly Cousins took the union through its post-war social and political revolution and in a very real sense can be said to have paved the way, eventually, for men like Bill Morris to succeed. Indeed he became, and remained, a role model adopted by

Morris. It is no exaggeration to suggest that without this extraordinary transformation in the socio-political character of the TGWU the Bill Morris phenomenon might never have occurred. If Bevin was the genius who founded and built the union, then equally it was the genius, and courage, of Cousins who transformed the TGWU to what it eventually became, the trade union powerhouse for radical social and political reform across the entire British Labour Movement.

The Cousins 'revolution' inside (and outside) the TGWU began with a revival of rank and file opinion. Shop-floor workers across the union were given a freedom of expression they had not experienced since the earliest days of Bevin's creation. Factory-level democracy was encouraged explicitly from the very top of this huge union, then with about 1.3 million members and expanding. Strike action which generally had been anathema during the reign of Arthur Deakin (and even in Bevin's later stages) was legitimised when and where deemed necessary. A new political dimension was created by Cousins when he pledged the TGWU to support nuclear disarmament despite fierce opposition from the Labour Party leadership, then under Hugh Gaitskell, as well as most of Cousins's fellow union leaders.

Cousins was fearless and determined to create a new political and industrial platform of radical policies. When Gaitskell died he was succeeded as Labour leader by Harold Wilson – indeed it was Frank Cousins and the T&G who played a prominent part in ensuring

Wilson's succession against other contenders. When Wilson became Prime Minister after the 1964 general election he invited Frank Cousins to join his cabinet as the nation's first Minister of Technology. It was a prime role in a new and innovative department of government and no doubt Wilson saw a possible parallel with Attlee's 1945 appointment of Bevin in having a powerful trade union figure in his cabinet. The new Prime Minister believed that by bringing Cousins into government and finding him a Parliamentary seat he would fill a vital gap in the structure of the new cabinet. Cousins was 'found' a safe seat in the Midlands constituency of Nuneaton, but he was never comfortable within the culture and ambience of the House of Commons and much like Bevin he found Parliamentary life irritating with its theatrical mock dignity completely different from the rough and tumble and hurly-burly of trade union life. Bevin was more fortunate in having gained his Parliamentary experience under wartime conditions – though he never lost his disdain for the Parliamentary process. Cousins tried hard to improve on Bevin's Parliamentary style but was not a successful minister and in 1966 resigned after nearly two years in government to return to his real love – leading the TGWU.

In the few remaining years he had before retirement Cousins masterminded his succession by ensuring that it would go to his selected man – Jack Jones, an exceptionally talented union organiser who had deliberately been kept at arm's length and in a lower role within the TGWU during Deakin's reign as general secretary. James Larkin Jones, son of a Liverpool docker, was a left-wing rebel who had fought with the International Brigade against Franco's fascist armies during the Spanish Civil War in which he was wounded. He returned to Britain, became a full-time official of the TGWU with a junior job in Coventry where he spent the war years organising with remarkable success for the union. By any normal standards he would have been promoted to national office at the end of the war but Deakin stamped on that because Jones remained a committed Leftist. It was only when Cousins became leader of the union that the doors were re-opened for Jones as a new democratic spirit swept the union. Jones became secretary for the important Midlands region of the TGWU before Cousins brought him to the union's London headquarters as an assistant secretary: that was a calculated move to prime Jones for eventual succession. In the meantime a young black man, Bill Morris, had joined the TGWU in Birmingham, having caught the attention of some of Jack Jones's lieutenants in the area. The young Morris, working as a semi-skilled engineering worker for Hardy Spicer, manufacturers of automobile parts, had risen to shop steward status in Hardy Spicer's Birmingham plant and was already being encouraged to consider a career as a full-time official in Britain's largest trade union. However, by then Frank Cousins, already an iconic figure in Morris's perception, had retired to take on the role as the first chairman of a newly created Race Relations Commission, a role that reflected

Cousins's long-standing commitment to racial equality. Again this proved to be a symbolic step in favour of Bill Morris.

The Commission was established in November 1968, a few months before Cousins's retirement from the TGWU so, initially, he was appointed as part-time chairman. The Commission itself took over the functions of the former National Committee for Commonwealth Immigrants, which had been formed in 1965 by Harold Wilson's government. A parallel though somewhat different body, the Race Relations Board, had already been created under an earlier Race Relations Act of 1965. But the aim in creating a new Race Relations Commission was to broaden the whole approach to handling the problems inherent in race relations affairs. The prime function of the Commission under Cousins became one of education, publicity and exhortation: to spread a liberal humanitarian message across British society to demonstrate the advantages of immigration and seek to disseminate goodwill and greater mutual understanding to ease racial tensions within all communities. That suited the idealistic character of Cousins but it did not resolve the bureaucratic problems inherent in having two separate organisations dealing with race relations. Cousins spent most of his time as chairman of the Commission trying to bring the two organisations together under one umbrella. That may well have happened but for the intervention of a general election in June 1970 which Wilson lost, bringing a Conservative government to Westminster under the leadership of Edward Heath. All of this happened in less than a year following Cousins's appointment as chairman of the Commission. The new home secretary Reginald Maudling wanted to pick up the threads left over by the Wilson government. The new Conservative minister was sympathetic towards the entire process and got on well with Cousins and was ready to work in close co-operation with him. But there were too many tensions within both the Commission and the Race Relations Board that left Cousins, the idealist fighting to make swift progress, deeply frustrated. These problems both between and within the two organisations often reflected racial tensions in the country at large. Cousins found the whole atmosphere dispiriting and unnecessary and finally decided to resign and chose to go into retirement. Yet he never lost his faith or his conviction in the need to fight against racial intolerance and discrimination. However his health was already showing signs of weakening and he never fully regained enough physical strength to resume public life. Even so he had left an indelible mark across the race relations field almost as profound and as influential as his contribution in the trade union world. He had effectively prepared new ground for Bill Morris to tread.

It was during the reign of Cousins's successor Jack Jones as general secretary of the TGWU that Bill Morris became a full-time official. As with Cousins, racial equality was always high on the agenda for Jack Jones. He was unstinting in his support for Cousins at the

Race Relations Commission and that support remained long after Cousins went into retirement at the end of 1970. Nor did it waver under Jones's successor when he retired. He was followed by Moss Evans, on whose watch Bill Morris rose to become a national official of the union. Still more dramatically it was under Evans's successor Ron Todd that Bill Morris would finally ascend to the leadership of the union. It was Todd, the former Ford car worker from London's East End and a radical in the Cousins mould, who became a fervent admirer of Morris. It was Todd, a committed socialist, who eventually created the opportunity for Bill Morris to take over as general secretary when he retired and it was Todd who fought consistently against racial prejudices within the union. With his streak of Cousins-style determination Ron Todd overcame the obstacles. None of this was easy; none of it would have been possible without the earlier pathways having been prepared by leaders who were determined to change the culture, the practices and the morality of the vast assembly called the Transport and General Workers Union. It was a combined operation, to be sure, although an operation fortunate to have been led by a group of men for whom the colour of skin would never become an obstacle to the progress of people of talent. Much of this was the legacy of the Cousins 'revolution'; but also, inescapably, of changing social mores across Britain.

2

Roots and Survival

IF THIS BOOK WERE BEING CRAFTED as a novel then its main character could hardly be better introduced than by describing the origins and early experiences of Bill Morris. Nor can I think of a better author in such an enterprise than Gabriel García Márquez, that master of the canvas embracing the complexities of Spanish culture across Latin America. For there is enough Spanish influence in the historic background of the West Indies, where Bill Morris was born and spent his earliest teenage years, to provide Márquez with all the material he might need. Like so much in that zone there is a deep history of Spanish power, influence and culture in the entire Caribbean.

Long years after Spain conceded control, influence and even specific interest in the region there remained, and still remains, an unmistakable Spanish *pasticcio*. Of course the centuries have shifted the scenery and for the young Morris it was essentially the years of British presence, and power, in Jamaica that nurtured and influenced his childhood and prepared him for the road ahead.

Even so it would be an error to ignore the deeper background involved in the savage history of the Caribbean region. As we travel back in time before British imperial rule became the dominant influence on an already imported slave trade of African immigrants, there is no questioning the prime influence of Spain with its pioneering spirit of Imperial plunder and use of slave labour across the whole region.

Move back across the centuries to 1494 to the discovery of the Caribbean by Columbus and his partners, the Piazon brothers. Here lay the true origins of Spanish imperialism across the region, which established a domination lasting more than a century before the English and the French even began to penetrate the zone and loosen Spain's grip. This is not intended as offering a detailed history of the battles that raged across the Caribbean and spread over three centuries of imperial rivalry between the developing sea powers of Spain, France and Britain, however it is important to appreciate the pivotal role played by the slave trade in colonising what we now call the West Indies. It is important to recognise this history as a backcloth to the Bill Morris story. Indeed it was the slave trade, opened up by the Spaniards, that set the pattern for what followed across the centuries.

Spain fell increasingly behind the British and French in developing the expanding trans-Atlantic slave trade but not before the Spaniards had laid a foundation stone for economic exploitation and trading. Yet like so many pioneers Spain suffered the fate of having to compete with latecomers who were better equipped and probably better organised in the process of global slave trading. In no sense was the conduct of the British and French any less brutally opportunist than the Spanish; they simply managed a developing technology of the age more skilfully or perhaps with more ruthless efficiency. British and French sea power gradually overtook and overpowered the competition. Their ships were more advanced, innovative and improving rapidly – an important factor in the early imperial rivalry and its accompanying parallel, the fierce contest for economic supremacy. Above all it was this bitter fight for control along the slave trade shipping routes of the Atlantic as they opened the gateways to the 'New World' that effectively established an Anglo-French supremacy and intensified the rivalry between Britain and France. It also laid the foundations for what was to become the African-American 'problem' and ultimately the American Civil War. So, without drawing too deeply from this complex well of history it is important to recognise the influences of all these elements in shaping what eventually became the British West Indies.

For it was in Jamaica, where the British finally established themselves in 1655, that the island colony became a major base for the slave market covering the entire region. Before that Spain had created an early garrison in Jamaica in 1509 but then began using their range of

Caribbean bases as springboards for more ambitious moves across Latin America in general, notably to invade and conquer Mexico. That left Spain overstretched and vulnerable to raiding parties carrying the flags of Britain and France while at the same time Spanish troops also faced constant revolt from the natives of the Caribbean – the Arawak Indians –whom they had started to use as slaves to mine gold in the region, notably on islands such as Haiti (then called Hispaniola). As Spain's hold over all their island conquests gradually weakened the British moved into the settlements of St Kitts, Barbados, Antigua and Montserrat, while the French set up shop in Martinique, Guadeloupe and Dominica. By the seventeenth century Spain had already ceded large areas to the British and French and the real fight to develop economic imperialism was about to reach a peak.

The prime attraction for all three imperial powers was to gain access and control over a potentially vast area of mineral and agricultural wealth. There was gold in the hills, for sure; but equally as important were the then still developing sugar plantations. There was a prime incentive to develop these plantations that were situated in the rich agricultural soil of the Caribbean and were also seen correctly as a vast potential storehouse. With the use of slave labour to exploit these riches the entire zone became a major base for international commerce. It had long been clear that the future of the international sugar trade depended largely on the use of black slave labour and it was the combination of these

two factors that turned the Caribbean into a commanding global economic area equal in contemporary terms
to the power of Middle East oil hegemony. Sugar was
a basic ingredient in the expanding food and liquor
trades of Europe. By the time the British and French
seized Spanish bases the original native Arawak Indian
population had already been decimated by disease and
brutal exploitation. This meant that the principal hurdle to expansion was an acute labour shortage to work
the sugar riches – a problem resolved by stepping up
the import of black slaves from Africa.

The imperial conflicts between Britain, France and
Spain continued into the eighteenth century through to
1794 and the French Revolution. By then the British had
already secured their strength over most of the Caribbean islands, though the French remained a powerful
competitive force until the fall of Napoleon. By then
Jamaica, under British control, had become a major base
and virtual headquarters for the region's slave trade. By
the middle of the nineteenth century Spanish control in
the Caribbean had been marginalised – though it still
left Spain with dominance over Cuba and Puerto Rico
and with strong influence in Mexico along with other
areas of Latin America. The Spanish-American wars at
the end of the nineteenth century finally turned the tide
on Spanish power in the zone forcing Spain to concede
Puerto Rico, Cuba, the Philippines and Guam (in the
Pacific) to the USA. Yet it was the British who remained
the predominant imperial power in the Caribbean –
with Jamaica as the Crown headquarters.

With the cultivation of sugar cane and coffee plus African slave labour Jamaica became one of the most valuable possessions in the world. Again the parallel in contemporary terms with the Middle East in respect of oil is an irresistible comparison. With Jamaica playing such a key role in this power game it is interesting to note that, at the time, the colony's slave population outnumbered the white [British] settlers by twenty to one. In this situation it is hardly surprising that the white settlers' domination was frequently challenged by uprisings and savage battles between the slaves and their masters with some of the disturbances threatening to destabilise the accumulating wealth as well as the safety of the white rulers. To try to control the plantations the settlers established a corps of 'black slave guards' – known as the Maroons – who were seduced and bribed to work with their masters to protect and police the plantations, against their own people. This suppression worked up to a point – although violence across the plantations never ceased until slavery was abolished in 1834. Even then Jamaican slaves remained bound to serve their former owners for many years, albeit with some minimum rights, until a more humane and liberal system was slowly introduced. In 1866 Jamaica was given the status of a Crown Colony with a measure of self-government though it wasn't until 1944 that the island gained a degree of local political control. What finally triggered this advancement toward political liberty were the strikes and riots of sugar workers and dockers in 1938, shortly before the outbreak of the

Second World War. These civil uprisings forced concessions from the British which effectively led to the
formation of Jamaica's first local political parties – the
Peoples' National Party (formed in 1938) and its rival,
the Jamaican Labour Party (launched a year later) –
developments which threw up Jamaica's most famed
political figures, Norman Washington Manley QC* and
William Alexander Bustamente.† Then in 1958 after the

---

* Norman Washington Manley QC (1893–1969). He was a cousin
of Bustamente but with a different background. He founded the
People's National Party and the National Workers Union after
the 1938 troubles. He became Chief Minister from 1955 to 1959
and then Prime Minister from 1959 to 1962 when Jamaica won its
status as an independent member of the Commonwealth. Manley
was educated at Oxford where he was a brilliant Rhodes Scholar
winning high honours in law studies. His parentage was mixed,
with both black and white family members on his mother's side.
His son Michael Manley succeeded his father to lead the Peoples'
National Party in 1969 on the death of Norman Manley. He too
became Prime Minister serving twice in 1972–1980 and again in
1989–1992.

† William Alexander Bustamente (1884–1977) was more of a
militant firebrand than his cousin Norman Manley and did not
have Manley's academic qualifications. He was an activist from
the start and became the leading labour and trade union figure
in Jamaica by creating the Bustamente Industrial Trade Union in
January 1939 after the 1938 riots. Within four years Bustamente's
union represented eighty per cent of the colony's organised
workers. But from September 1939 till February 1942 he was
imprisoned by Jamaica's governor Sir Arthur Richards for sedition
and released only after a trial in which his cousin Norman Manley
was his leading advocate. Then in December 1944 after Jamaica's

Second World War, in which many Jamaicans served in Britain's armed forces, Jamaica joined with nine other Caribbean islands to form the Federation of the West Indies. The Federation was short-lived and eventually, in 1962, Jamaica gained independence as a member of the Commonwealth.

Bill Morris was a child of this history. He grew up listening to the fiery doctrines of political independence and a peoples' representative democracy from Bustamente and Manley, especially the former; and, to be sure, an awareness that he was the product of an African background and like all other products of that history felt an emotional involvement. What is worth mentioning as a milestone is that the very year of Morris's birth, 1938, was the same year that civil unrest swept across the island with workers' revolts and strikes on the plantations and all the vital dockland areas.

On 19 October 1938 Bill Morris was born in a small village called Bombay, in the parish of Manchester, some sixty miles from the capital Kingston, a village near where his father William Morris and his mother

---

first general election (for limited self-government] Bustamente's Labour Party won twenty-three of the thirty-two seats in the new House of Representatives and he became Jamaica's first Chief Minister. He remained in that role until 1955 when his cousin Norman Manley was elected. Then in 1962 when full independence was conceded Bustamente took over from Manley as Prime Minister. By then the two cousins had fallen out and become strong opponents.

Una were born. His parents' village was Porus, the same region in which his grandparents had grown up and worked the plantations. The village of Bombay and its environs was, and remains, a small community with its own Baptist church and school – a village to which the now Lord Bill Morris of Handsworth will, occasionally, return though not to parade his elevated role as Chancellor of Kingston University and holder of the Order of Jamaica, an honour equivalent to a British knighthood given to Jamaicans of outstanding distinction, but rather to satisfy a deep emotional attachment to his roots.

When Bill Morris was a small child his mother remarried after the death of his father and the family moved to the even smaller village of Mizpah where there was a strong religious community based on the Moravian Church. His stepfather, Martin Luther Williams, had connections with that village and the Church and Bill's mother Una quickly became involved in working with the Moravian Church community, a devout Protestant group originating from Bohemia (in 1457) with a long record of evangelical missionary work in the Caribbean. Originally the founders of this religious grouping were followers of the Czech martyr Jan Huss. After being driven out of Bohemia the Church was restored in eighteenth-century Saxony and specialised in sending missionaries to the Americas. They also established a small base in the centre of London – in Fetter Lane off Fleet Street – but this was used primarily as a springboard for missionaries en route for North America and the Caribbean. It was with the Moravian Church in the tiny village of Mizpah, Jamaica, that the young Bill Morris first found his inspirational moral influences. Guided by his grandmother and his mother and the local Minister, the Reverend. S. U. Hastings – who subsequently became Bishop of Kingston – Morris was steered by the ethical code of the Church and his family. The basis of this code was quite simply one of social help to less fortunate neighbours. Young Morris was especially influenced by his mother Una who was active not only with the Church, but in general social work throughout the village, often at her own initiative. The Morris's were not poverty-stricken. They were poor but hard-working with their own little smallholding. No member of the Morris/Williams family went short of food, much of it produced from their own small-holding with the surplus going to local markets. Bill's stepfather was also well connected and apart from his farming activity he worked part-time as a volunteer with the local police constabulary. It was by no means an unhappy home. Bill had a good relationship with his stepfather, a kindly generous man, though it was his mother Una and his maternal grandmother who were the prime influences throughout his childhood. Una, the ardent churchgoer, masterminded a practical moral agenda for the whole family; she was intent on young Bill having the best possible education – not just from the village primary school but also, where necessary, by paying for extra tuition.

Reflecting on that childhood Lord Bill now observes: 'My mother was always very ambitious for me: she insisted on my having extra lessons. But I have to admit that as soon as school finished at four p.m. in the afternoon all I was really interested in was playing cricket. That was my main interest. I loved the game and my great hero as a child was George Headley*… I wanted to be like him; cricket was part of my life … sometimes, looking back, I think it was part of all our lives.' In fact Bill's overwhelming ambition as he entered his teens was to become a professional cricketer and play for his country, the West Indies. 'Oh, sure, I was happy at school and I enjoyed those young days in my community.' He reflects back to that community with glowing pride. 'There was a spirit of co-operation and sense of community. People helped each other – maybe it was a reflection of so many people involved in work in the fields, harvesting and all that; it typified the spirit of

---

* George Alphonso Headley was one of the finest batsmen of all time. He played for Kingston and Jamaica and was twenty-two times capped by the West Indies Test team between 1930 and 1954 finishing with a test average of 60.83, the third highest in cricket history after Don Bradman. He died in 1983 aged seventy-four. Bill Morris named his two sons, Clyde and Garry, after famous cricketers; Clyde Arthur Morris (born 27 November 1957) was named after the famous Australian batsman Arthur Morris. His younger brother Garry Alexander Morris (born 18 November 1958) was named after a famous Jamaican wicket keeper and Test team captain Franz C. M. Alexander (Test career 1957–1961), though there also a touch of the great Garry (Garfield) Sobers in that name as well.

co-operation. And that's what I admired so much about cricket – it contained a great sense of co-operation, a kind of kindred spirit.'

Bill Morris is a shy man and he confesses to a mix of conflicting emotions when making occasional visits to his birthplace, Bombay, and the village of Mizpah which contain most of his boyhood memories. To be sure he feels a touch out of place though he remains deeply attached to his roots. For a long time he privately held onto the ownership of his mother's (and grand-mother's) old home in Mizpah – he now admits 'out of pure sentiment'. With reluctance he sold it ten years ago and now says: 'I wanted to hold onto my childhood memories. I confess I have, and always have had, a tre-mendous emotional attachment to that place.'

As many great philosophers and writers have argued, it is our childhood which holds the key to the myster-ies of character and it would be hard to find a better example of this than in the story of Bill Morris. What Rousseau, Wordsworth, Freud and so many other ana-lysts have observed is the enduring significance of our earliest experiences and an inescapable truth that this indelible mark remains with us for the rest of our lives.

Bill Morris left school at fourteen but didn't imme-diately seek a job. He remained around the home for quite a while after leaving school chiefly to help his wid-owed mother but also, in his own words, 'because I just bummed around a bit'. After the death of his stepfather,

Martin Luther Williams, Morris knew that his mother needed his presence: she was, as ever, the strongest influence in his life. But there was also the prevailing influence of cricket; the magnetic lure of the game he loved and which became almost obsessive. All his spare moments were given to playing in a local team and with at least one eye on the possibility of becoming a professional cricketer. It was very much his lifestyle in the immediate months after leaving school and may well have remained the dominant feature had his mother not decided on a move which was destined to transform Bill Morris's entire life and circumstances.

Having lost two husbands Una Williams decided to join a brother who earlier had emigrated to England. She wanted to break with an experience she had known since birth and try her luck with the wave of emigration that had begun to cross the Atlantic during the early 1950s in the first flush of what was to become a huge cultural shift.* To the people in the communities of Bombay and Mizpah, England remained a symbolic name across the ocean, a country far removed from the Caribbean culture in which the Morris family were reared. It also beckoned a new and perhaps more prosperous future. In search of that difference Una Williams

---

* Una Williams was in fact part of the early influx of immigrants from the Caribbean. The first large group of post-war immigrants from the West Indies arrived in June 1948 at Tilbury on the ship *Empire Windrush*. There were 492 registered immigrants from Jamaica.

came to Birmingham, England while her fifteen-year-old son Bill remained behind ... at least for the time being.

With his mother in England and living with her brother in Birmingham Bill Morris found it hard to remain in Mizpah without her so he moved to Kingston where his stepsister lived with her husband. His sister's husband worked on a building site in the Jamaican capital and he helped to find work for Bill as an apprentice plasterer. For over a year Bill Morris worked alongside his stepbrother-in-law on various building developments in the rapidly expanding capital – cinemas, hospitals, schools – and became a competent plasterer. He also picked up a basic knowledge of the building industry in general which in later years he would find useful. But he was increasingly restless. He greatly missed his mother and eventually was driven to the obvious conclusion – to follow in her footsteps to Birmingham. So he quit his building job, said goodbye to his stepsister and her husband and in November 1954, aged just sixteen, Bill Morris arrived in England. When he reflects back to that moment he remembers how nervous he felt; indeed so nervous and unsure that he didn't want to leave the plane. Finally he summoned the courage to walk off – into the waiting, welcoming arms of his mother who had travelled to Heathrow by coach from Birmingham to meet him. It was a memorable reunion. That evening they both returned to Birmingham by coach.

Una Williams had settled in a large house in the Handsworth area of Birmingham. It was a district in the north-west of the city which had once been the residential zone for the developing middle classes at the end of the nineteenth century. As the prosperity of Britain's second-largest city grew during the First World War Handsworth was a desirable suburb but gradually it moved down-market and by the early fifties had already become a base for a large West Indies immigrant population. Immigrant families took over the old and large Victorian houses for multi-lettings. By the early 1960s whole families, sub-families and friends within the immigrant population dominated the area, often sharing the same accommodation. Racial tension grew and there was some street rioting in the sixties, though less violent than in other parts of Britain.

The most vivid impressions of his first introduction to Handsworth remain in Bill Morris's mind. But they were not about racial tension. It was his baptism to a completely different culture and environment: 'I shall never forget my first real sight of Handsworth. On the morning after my arrival I woke up and pulled back the curtain to look out across the landscape. I couldn't believe my eyes. Everything, but everything, was different. In front of me was a landscape the like of which I had never before seen – of grey houses with chimney pots, all exuding clouds of smoke. I remember saying to myself as I looked out across that grey landscape, seeing smoke oozing out of hundreds of chimney stacks … I recall saying to myself … surely they can't all be on fire …'

No, there was no huge fire; it was Handsworth, Birmingham, on a normal grim, grey autumn morning long before smokeless zones had been considered. Morris's description paints the picture: 'I had never before seen houses with chimneys with smoke pouring out of them like that. In Jamaica the houses are mainly of wood with plaster-coated concrete blocks. That morning, as I looked with disbelief across that Birmingham landscape I realised then that I was in a foreign land … It was a stunning impact that I can never forget.'

It was his first significant realisation that his life had now changed for ever. He knew then that he was in a different land.

The environment may have been that of a foreign land to Bill Morris but he was back with his mother, which provided an immense level of comfort. His uncle, Una's brother, had already established himself in Birmingham and was working with the General Electric Company in another district of the city. He succeeded in persuading his management to find a job for his young nephew and this was how the sixteen-year-old immigrant started his first job in England as a lowest grade general hand for GEC. Working on the bottom rung of the ladder was certainly no honeymoon for the young man still trying to adjust to life in a strange land with a completely new social environment. His job was, in truth, mindless dogsbody work that involved doing anything and everything at the whim of a disinterested and no doubt racialist shop foreman – tea-making, carrying loads, running errands and so on. Even so it was a job and he tried to be realistic about it. As Morris now describes that first work experience in Britain: 'It was a soul-destroying job for which I was paid four pounds a week [about a quarter the average pay at that time] but it was my first job in England and I was glad to have it.' It didn't last long. Under his own steam he quickly found alternative work with a small engineering firm not far from his Handsworth home and he remained in that job for eight months. The environment was quite different from that in his previous job – it was friendly and surprisingly hospitable, not least because the workforce consisted mostly of women doing semi-skilled work who were well disposed towards the young immigrant. They helped pass on to Bill some of their skills such as how to grind and drill metals, though there was no structured apprenticeship scheme; even so he was able to pick up the threads of those skills. Most of all he found the workforce warm and helpful and got on well with most of them. 'They mothered and spoiled me,' he now reflects, 'and they were so warmly helpful that some of them actually clubbed together to lend me some money to buy a bike … my very first bicycle … and then later they even helped buy my very first suit.' His wage packet was still only a few pounds a week – he thinks it was about double what he had been getting before. Yet he managed to save a bit which helped out at home – though his mother ensured the home was not an impoverished one. Una worked hard and was always able to find a job. At first she worked at a small engineering works but later found a job at one of Birmingham's main hospitals. She was tenacious at keeping up a comfortable home for the family, devoted to young Bill and setting a high standard of social and ethical behaviour.

At work in his new job with its agreeable feminine ambience Bill Morris was not conscious of any racial tension. 'Not a thing,' he says. 'They were exceptionally good to me. Frankly, looking back at that period I often feel that working for that small engineering firm in that friendly environment with no racial tension that I was aware of was one of the happiest times of my life. All thanks to the wonderful friendly spirit of those workmates. I had never had anything like that before. But after eight months with that firm they decided to move to a new plant outside Birmingham. I didn't want to move away from home again so I had to find a new job. Even so I had been able to save enough money to pay off my debts to the girls at the factory for their loans … '

Then came his next job – with a firm he managed to stay with until he became a full-time official with the Transport and General Workers Union. Hardy Spicer was a large engineering firm based in Erdington, Birmingham. It was part of a wider group and well known as an important producer of parts for motor cars and trucks. Morris succeeded in getting that job simply by going to the plant and, literally, knocking on their door. It was a lucky break – though at first he was a touch reluctant to take the job because Erdington was a fair distance from his Handsworth home. He overcame these doubts by reckoning he could use his precious bike to bridge the travel problem. It was a move that was to set the foundation stone on which the rest of his career was built. He began work with Hardy Spicer towards the end of 1956. Bill, then eighteen, was beginning to settle in his own mind and slowly gaining in self-confidence. He remained with the company for eighteen years before finally moving on in 1973 to become a full-time official of the union. Ironically it was a trade union he had not rushed to join when he started at Hardy Spicer; yet it was the organisation which eventually was to become his life-time career, carrying him on to a unique position in British society.

3

Starting Life in Britain

THE EARLY FORMATIVE YEARS WORKING at the Hardy Spicer plant in Erdington contained many of the ingredients that went to shape the future life and career of Bill Morris. It was a critical period for him and was reflected in his oft-used quote in later years when asked about his starting point: 'I am very much a product of the shop floor.' It is an important point since it offers a revealing insight into one of the characteristics that remained with Morris throughout his career. There was always a self-effacing tendency to understate his capacity rather than capitalise on achievements; a tendency in effect to say: 'I will prove myself in my work not by words.' Perhaps reflecting an ultra-sensitive awareness that boastful claims could invite unstated racial sneers.

Of course he was slowly adjusting to an entirely different culture. He was gaining in self-confidence after a few years on the shop floor at Hardy Spicer and was well aware of the general undertone of racialism not only at work but in the city generally. He had arrived in Birmingham at a time when racial tensions between native Brummies and the immigrant West Indian community were moving to street conflicts, especially on weekend evenings. On Friday and Saturday nights local white groups would gather to beat up black youngsters. Insults, obscenities would be flung across the street and followed by physical violence, with fists and sometimes more sinister weapons.

Bill Morris was nearing his eighteenth birthday when he started work at Hardy Spicer and he had already experienced both sides of the racial scene; the warm hospitable helpfulness of the largely female workforce in his earlier small engineering plant, and the local street tensions in Handsworth and surrounding districts of Birmingham, where a young black face was often enough to invite trouble. The contrast troubled and puzzled him. Reflecting back on that formative period he says: 'The truth was that the whole racial situation was effectively a battle for survival – a battle for existence. You need to remember that the black community at that time had no political muscle; no public voice. Teddy boys would beat up the black lads on a Saturday night, especially after the pubs closed in Birmingham. That was when trouble started and we black kids knew we must be at home to avoid trouble.'

So what was it like when he began working at Hardy Spicer? Was he aware of these tensions on the shop floor? 'Yes, there was prejudice though most of the people I worked with at the time were quite tolerant.

The prejudice often manifested itself in the form of sly jokes, typical of working-class humour and maybe typical also of Brummie culture. Black workers were fully aware that things were being said about them but we all tolerated it in a kind of light-hearted way and with a shrug of the shoulders. We hadn't much choice … We simply didn't have the self-confidence to challenge any of that prejudice. It wasn't so much that we were acquiescing, it was more of a shrugging acceptance of reality. And that attitude applied across most of the black community – whether in the workplace or among society in general.'

When the young Bill Morris was assailed, as sometimes he was, with the remark 'Go home you black bastard', he replied with a simple 'But I am at home', and walked away. He always sought to avoid conflict.

Every aspect of life and living was overshadowed by these tensions. Most notable of all was the problem of housing new immigrants. Multiple occupation was the norm – in Handsworth as elsewhere; the sharing of homes with extended families and friends was common practice. As Morris describes it: 'Often complete strangers from the immigrant community would suddenly appear in the next bed to me at home. Sometimes it might be a friend of the family or someone who had been recommended to stay with us for a time. Of course this was part of the solidarity among black immigrants trying to help each other.'

One of the concomitant problems endemic in such a situation was exploitation by members of their own community – black immigrants who somehow had managed to acquire enough capital to buy up older houses and rent them at extortionate rates. Morris again reflects: 'They would buy a house, usually in a very poor run-down condition and then sublet rooms to exploit their own people. Life was tough for sure ...'

Many of the multi-occupation houses had limited sanitation and toilet facilities. Like most of his generation Bill Morris would go to the local public baths every Saturday for a complete clean-up. 'I usually went there on my way back home after working a half-day Saturday shift,' he says.

But working at Hardy Spicer helped to cushion some of the tougher moments of life for young Morris. He liked the job, worked hard and was accepted by his shop-floor mates. The company made prop shafts and universal joints for motor cars, trucks and buses and Bill worked as a machine operator in a section of the plant producing these parts for buses. He also signed up to start day release courses in engineering at the Handsworth Technical College – another pointer to his determined effort to merge into the new work and life culture of his adopted country.

Within a few weeks of joining the firm he was also approached to sign up with a trade union – the Transport and General Workers. There were in fact four unions active in the Hardy Spicer plant of which the National Union of Metal Mechanics was the largest. The other unions were the engineers and a white-collar trade union called APEX. But, without hesitation,

Morris opted for the TGWU. It was his first and only trade union. But more importantly Bill Morris had just married. About a year after starting with Hardy Spicer Bill Morris met Minetta Smith in his mother's house in Handsworth, where Minetta's family were renting accommodation. It happened by chance one day when he returned from work to find a strikingly attractive girl standing in front of the fire in his mother's living room. Minetta was introduced as the daughter of the family who had moved in ... and that was it. Bill claims it was love at first sight. They married after a brief, highly romantic, courtship of which he now says, 'I fell in love straight away.' Apart from the special relationship with his mother and his grandmother it was the marriage with Minetta, who was slightly older, that played a crucial role in moulding his life, as he frequently ruminates: 'It was these three women who have really influenced my life.'

Their first son Clyde Arthur Morris was born in November 1957 and their second son, Garry Alexander, exactly one year later.

So there he was – just twenty years old, married with two small children, still fresh in a new job and learning the skills of his trade by conscientious attendance at weekly classes. There was little spare time for trade union work and indeed Bill Morris showed no enthusiasm to become active in his union for another four years – and even then the launch was largely accidental or, at best, casual. A natural shyness contributed to holding him back.

In the end he was drawn into union activity chiefly because of a shop-floor demand for an improvement in health and safety conditions for workers. The specific issue which triggered his own involvement was a request for protective clothing which reached a climax at a moment when the department's shop steward was absent ill. Morris was persuaded by his shop-floor mates to stand in for the absent shop steward to help negotiate with management for improved safety conditions, especially in supplying protective clothing. So the reluctant, shy, Bill Morris was catapulted into the role by common consent of his workmates. He succeeded in persuading management to concede the shop-floor demands, though Morris now claims: 'To this day I cannot remember how I stated the case, but there it is; the shop-floor argument was accepted and when the regular shop steward returned after his sick leave he told me he didn't wish to continue as a steward. So my shop-floor mates asked me if I would take on the role permanently – and I agreed.' The management were far from union-friendly; they tolerated the trade unions and recognised their status only when they had to. So his new role as shop steward in 1963 was no easy task, and indeed within a year he was involved in his first big industrial dispute. One of the convenors in the company had been dismissed. Sacking a convenor of shop stewards – in effect, the leader of a shop stewards grouping – amounts to a major challenge by any employer and predictably it led to a strike at Hardy Spicer which lasted several weeks. The dispute happened to erupt shortly before the 1964 general election and inevitably became entangled with the politics of the moment. Morris recalls how the company chairman, Herbert Hill, inflamed the conflict by making a gratuitous remark about his own workforce: 'He made a very patronising comment about his own workers – describing them as "poor dears". That remark was so insulting to the shop floor since it implied the men were being led by the nose and were not responsible for their own actions. It toughened resolve and the strike ended with the convenor being re-instated and the union fully recognised. Shortly afterwards the company chairman resigned.' It was a valuable experience for Bill Morris.

The incoming Labour government in the autumn of 1964 under Harold Wilson brought another important landmark for Morris. He was twenty-six and maturing in his trade union role. He was also by then an established employee of the company. In fact his abilities were being noticed not only by local trade union officials but equally by the Hardy Spicer management. He even began to contemplate the possibility of promotion within the company's developing managerial structure. He thought an offer might be in the offing for him to take on a supervisory role on the shop floor – which would have been a remarkable move by the company given the racial tensions at that time. Yet by then the attraction of trade union work and his popularity as a shop steward had begun to have an even greater influence on his thinking. The general political environment was also conducive to encouraging his enthusiasm for trade unionism, notably the inspiring message offered by the new Prime Minister Harold Wilson who heralded the opportunities opening up in what he described as the 'white heat of the technological revolution'. Moreover Morris was getting vibes of strong support and encouragement from local full-time union officials of the TGWU and especially from one man in particular, George Wright, who was the district officer of the union in its Birmingham region engineering group. In fact Wright was also encouraged to foster and develop young Bill Morris by another leading figure in the TGWU Midlands region – Brian Mathers, the regional secretary. Mathers, a left-wing figure, was one of the beneficiaries of the union's shift towards a more radical political, industrial and social policy under its national leader Frank Cousins; and the name Cousins (then only a name to Morris) had increasingly attracted young Bill Morris. He had come to view Cousins as an inspirational leader not least because of the general secretary's views on racial affairs. Frank Cousins was of course already an established national trade union figure when Bill Morris began work with Hardy Spicer. From the moment he became general secretary of the TGWU in 1956 his dramatic impact on the political as well as the industrial scene was little short of exceptional. By the time the young Morris reached shop steward status Cousins was renowned as one of the very few national trade union leaders prepared to speak out with unusual courage in support of immigrant communities and black workers. The message was not lost on

Bill Morris. Frank Cousins became Morris's role model and remained so for the rest of his rise to the leadership of the TGWU where his greatest pride was then to find himself in the seat once held by his hero.

The period of the mid- to late-sixties was especially volatile for race relations in Britain. Tensions that had been simmering just below the surface for some years began to erupt into open conflict sometimes on the streets of towns and cities as well as in various industries where white workers felt their traditional culture was coming under threat. The Midlands was a particularly sensitive zone not least because outside the London area it attracted a larger number of African and Caribbean immigrants than most other areas in England. It was of course in the heartland of British industrial expansion. In Birmingham Bill Morris had already experienced these tensions but had learned to live with a social conflict that was unpleasant but not intolerable. The Labour government of Harold Wilson, elected in 1964 and re-elected with a larger overall majority in 1966, passed legislation that technically sought to make race discrimination illegal. Yet it was one thing for Parliament to pass new laws but quite another for those laws to become effective. The trade unions as a corporate entity were, again in theory, opposed to racial discrimination, with leaders like Frank Cousins playing a significant role as the head of the country's largest trade union.

However the opposition faced by Cousins and those

who shared his hopes and views did not diminish during his period of office nor for many years afterwards – indeed if then. One of the strongest manifestations of this racial tension in the sixties was the emergence of Enoch Powell as the key spokesman attacking the whole nature of immigration policy and offering himself effectively as the voice of the native white British population. Powell was the Conservative Party's MP for Wolverhampton south-west, a city in the heart of the industrial Midlands. He was also a former cabinet minister in the Macmillan Tory governments of the late fifties and early sixties. On Saturday, 20 April 1968, in Birmingham, Powell chose to make a speech loaded with dramatic and explosive racial content. That speech became a political sensation, and echoed across the entire race relations debate for years to come. Indeed, years after his death it remains a strong influence on racial attitudes. Powell's words are worth recalling especially since they were made at a critical time as Bill Morris was settling into the environment of working life in Britain. This is the explosive section from that speech:

'As I look ahead, I am filled with foreboding. Like the Roman, I seem to see "the River Tiber foaming with much blood". That tragic and intractable phenomenon which we watch with horror on the other side of the Atlantic but which there is interwoven with the history and existence of the States itself, is coming upon us here by our own volition and our own neglect. Indeed, it has all but come.

In numerical terms, it will be of American pro-
portions long before the end of the century.'

Three days after Powell made that speech the Wilson
government's Race Relations Bill was debated in the
House of Commons. Powell argued that the Bill raised
'offensive and immoral' issues. While Parliament was
debating the Bill an extraordinary demonstration took
place outside the House of Commons: about a thou-
sand London dockworkers marched to Westminster
in support of Enoch Powell, followed the next day
by some 400 porters from London's Smithfield meat
market, also in support of Powell and his views. The
majority of the dockers and the meat market porters
were members of the Transport and General Workers
Union whom, when challenged about their support for
the Tory Enoch Powell, responded with remarks such
as: 'He's English' and 'He's white'. In response to such
comments the official line from the TGWU sought to
minimise this damage. The union claimed that this
astonishing public support for Powell was not typical of
their London membership, that it had been fomented
and encouraged by fascist groups such as the National
Front, forerunner of the British National Party, and
that it was certainly not representative of general feeling among working people. The truth is more complex.
There can be little doubt that Powell's outburst was a
genuine, albeit gravely and dangerously exaggerated,
reflection of the unease already developing throughout white working-class communities about the scale

and impact of immigration. In later years this has been more widely recognised. For Powell himself it was effectively the end of a serious career in political life. Edward Heath who was then leader of the Conservative Party sacked Powell from the Tory shadow cabinet and he never again held another senior political post. In 1974 he resigned from the Conservative Party and his Wolverhampton seat. His reason at the time was his disagreement with Edward Heath over Tory Party policy towards Europe. Yet his 'Rivers of Blood' speech as it became labelled remained like a symbolic flag for Enoch Powell for the rest of his life. Indeed in the 1970 general election, two years after Powell's notorious speech, Edward Heath led the Conservatives to victory and it was claimed that Powell's views had been influential in at least some two and a half million votes switching to the Tories. Nonetheless Powell quit the party and became an MP for the Ulster Unionists in Northern Ireland and remained their Parliamentary man until 1987 when he lost the seat. He died aged eighty-five in February 1998, utterly unrepentant.

Why has it been important to outline this period from the late 1960s? Simply because it helps illustrate the political, social and cultural atmospherics of the time; a time when Bill Morris was being recognised by the TGWU as someone with serious potential talent. Cousins retired in 1969 to be succeeded by Jack Jones, very much a man of the Midlands despite his Merseyside origins. For it was in the industrial heartlands around Birmingham and Coventry that Jones had made his reputation as a national trade union figure. When after becoming general secretary he was advised first by Harry Urwin, his successor as Midlands regional secretary, and then by Urwin's successor Brian Mathers, that there was a black shop steward of talent and great promise Jones seized on this opportunity to demonstrate that his union could and would give a lead by promoting an active black trade unionist – even if this might be against the grain of some of his white membership. In effect the TGWU leadership, in the wake of Frank Cousins, had already decided to set an example to the rest of the Labour Movement in defiance of Enoch Powell and perhaps more significantly in defiance of what had happened among the dockers and meat porters who had supported Powell.

Effectively this developed from the enterprise and initiative of two of the union's key men in the Midlands: Brian Mathers, who became regional secretary in 1969 and one of his most prominent and able local officials, George Wright. The Midlands region was arguably the most important and influential section of the TGWU outside London – a focal point of the engineering and car industries. Mathers had been in charge of the engineering group in the area where he first spotted Bill Morris's rise to shop steward at Hardy Spicer. Yet probably even more important was the role of George Wright who took over from Mathers in running the engineering group for the region. It was Wright who really 'discovered' and helped develop Morris and alert both Mathers and then Urwin and

Jones in London to the potential in young Morris. It was Wright who observed Morris's early enthusiasm, his serious commitment to the trade union movement. Very few black workers were tempted to move into prominence whether as a trade union volunteer or in any role which might expose them to racial abuse. It was, and indeed remains, a long-standing problem in trying to encourage immigrant men and women to take up public positions, however modest the role. Both Mathers and George Wright were fully aware of this when they encouraged Morris to seek election to the Birmingham engineering district committee of the union, which consisted of some forty rank and file members under Wright's command. It was a highly important ingredient in Bill Morris's learning curve. And together Mathers and Wright continued to help Morris's development through to his eventual appointment as a full-time official of the union.

The most exciting moment at the very start of Bill Morris's climb to the top was probably Brian Mathers's support for him to attend the TGWU's prestigious biennial conference as a delegate from his local Birmingham branch No. 563. The conference, in July 1969 on the Isle of Man, was the farewell to Frank Cousins; he would retire in September of that year. It is not clear who first had the idea that it would be highly appropriate to have Morris as a delegate at the Cousins farewell conference. Various people have laid claim to that. It is said that Harry Urwin was the originator, perhaps conscious that he had discouraged an earlier proposal that Morris should be nominated for a full-time job as an official in the Midlands region on the grounds that the union was not yet ready for a full-time black officer. Urwin is said to have put the idea to Jack Jones who immediately approved. It is also suggested that the proposal initially came from Brian Mathers. Much more likely is that it was George Wright who pushed the idea at the outset. Whoever it was, there is no doubt it was an inspired initiative. Morris's first union biennial conference as a fully certified delegate was a memorable event in many respects. He was invited to present a retirement gift to his iconic man – Frank Cousins. In fact it turned out to be even more imaginative in that Morris was asked to shake hands with the general secretary and then present a retirement gift to his wife, Mrs Nance Cousins, to whom he handed a splendid sewing machine that had been a wish of both Frank and Nance Cousins. It was certainly a landmark moment for Bill Morris, and the handshake itself became a kind of talisman for him. He reflects on what it was about Cousins that inspired him so much: 'He stood out among all trade union leaders of the day. Of course I recognised that the TGWU was also special among trade unions – it was seen as the kingpin of the trade union movement. Yet it was really Cousins who attracted and influenced me … his courage and independence of mind; he was never a conformist; and I am not just referring to his views on racial issues. Compared with all other trade union leaders he simply stood out in every respect.' He never veered from that view and went on to try to use the Cousins model as his template when he finally became general secretary of the TGWU. When he did reach that position he played a prominent role in both arranging for a statue of Frank Cousins to be sculptured, which now stands in the foyer of the union's national head-quarters; and he also organised, along with Ron Todd, a periodic award of the union's 'Frank Cousins Peace Award' to the individual, or organisation in the Labour Movement making the most significant contribution to world peace.

As his status and experience developed in his role as shop steward and then as chairman of the engineering trade group for his region Morris attracted increasing notice from the senior officials of the Midlands region (the TGWU Region No.5 was one of its key areas). This was a time when the nation's biggest trade union had also become increasingly aware of the importance in recruiting the growing number of immigrant work-ers to trade unionism as well as its role as an exemplar, and which certainly became a factor in Bill Morris's rise from the shop floor. Mathers and Wright worked together on this agenda while making sure that Jones was kept aware at national level. But it was George Wright who played a crucial role. Wright himself had been a shop-floor worker in the car industry, working at the famed Austin Motors Longbridge plant, before he was appointed a full-time official. Wright was a highly experienced, yet still young, union official, his politics hovering around centre left, dedicated to building up shop-floor democracy within the TGWU. The name George Wright will reappear in an even more dramatic context later in this story – when, twenty years later, he was the favoured candidate for the general secretaryship of the union against his protégé, Bill Morris. The mentor who eventually was challenged and then defeated by his student. It was a remarkable twist to the story of the George Wright/Bill Morris relationship. However this is leaping ahead. In the late sixties Wright was still a relatively junior officer of the TGWU though already clearly in line for swift promotion. He was an extremely able, ambitious driving force. Even as a young official from the mid to late fifties he set about identifying around a hundred activists in his area. A number of Wright's selected few were black immigrants – part of his policy to encourage young black workers to become active in the union: Bill Morris was one of them, albeit the only black shop steward.

Various opportunities emerged for shop stewards of ability and commitment to apply for a job as a full-time union official. Having acquired a taste for trade unionism Morris, encouraged by Wright, would frequently be called on to stand in for a full-time official of the union who might be otherwise engaged. That would involve Morris negotiating with senior employers of the area, effecting the role of a paid official. Nor was this confined to the engineering trades. On one occasion Morris was asked to stand in for an official who had been scheduled to negotiate with the Cadbury company over wages and conditions at its famed Bourneville plant. So when a vacancy opened for a local district officer in Smethwick, near West Bromwich, Morris applied for the job, seeing it as an opportunity to put a foot on the bottom rung of the union's staffing ladder. Alas, it was the wrong place at the wrong time. It was shortly after the 1964 general election and the Smethwick constituency, hitherto a safe Labour area, had been thrown into a bitter racial battle which led to the defeat of the sitting member, Patrick Gordon Walker. He was a member of Wilson's shadow cabinet destined for a top ministerial post after the election but Gordon Walker was, quite sensationally, defeated by a local Conservative, Peter Griffiths, who campaigned against black immigration. Griffiths wanted to limit the number of black immigrants in Britain and especially in his home territory of Smethwick. This was still four years before Enoch Powell's 'Rivers of blood' speech. Of course Bill Morris knew when he applied for that Smethwick job that he would have been the first black person to be employed as a full-time official of the TGWU. He also knew that in the wake of the 1964 election result his chances of being appointed were at best minimal. In fact it was a no-win situation and his friends and mentors among Midlands region officials advised him to pull out. In particular it has been claimed that it was Harry Urwin, then Midlands region secretary, who held the view that it was too premature for Morris to apply for the Smethwick job. Whatever the truth of that suggestion, Morris was left with the impression that the attitude of senior officials was that the union was not yet ready for a full-time black officer and that Smethwick was not the place to start. He was advised to be patient and told 'your time will come'. After all Morris had been a shop steward for a mere two years. So he waited and continued to play an active role in the engineering trade group for the next few years. It was probably the memory of the Smethwick experience that later helped promote Morris's opportunities, notably his nomination to be a delegate at the union's conference of 1969. Two years after that he was also elected to the prestigious General Executive Council, the national policymaking body of the TGWU.

It was when he was initiated as a member of the national executive of the union that Morris first met Cousins's successor as general secretary, the formidable Jack Jones. That was an altogether different kind of baptism for the newcomer. The General Executive Council of the TGWU was a tough, frequently ruthlessly cunning, group of highly experienced lay members of the union over which Jones presided like a respected emperor. Yet even this commanding leader still had to contend with – and sometimes fight off – political and industrial ideas critical of his own position, regardless of his long reputation as a man of the Left. The composition of the union's executive was also strongly left-wing but that didn't exclude passionate rivalries between various factions of the Left. They were frequently divided into aggressive sects often pursuing narrow, and what might even be described as tribal, interests along with personal rivalries. Almost without exception the thirty-nine members of the General Executive Council prided themselves on their capacity to demonstrate independence, bloody-mindedness as well as a good measure of immodesty about their own debating skills. Any sign of weakness by Jones would have spelt chaos. His reputation as a tough, often ruthless leader became legendary. It was a style that enabled him to keep control over his hard-bitten executive. Morris witnessed all this with fascination – and with some inner anxiety. His own political stance at the time can best be described as centre left but he kept away from involvement in any of the rival groupings of the Left within the executive – which was never easy. When he did intervene he did so only after making sure he was well briefed on his subject. He knew he would need to stand up to tough interrogation. Morris was never close to Jack Jones. Indeed he found Jones an aloof figure, always demanding high standards and top performance from his executive members and discouraging superficial affability. Jones kept his distance. Few if any of his colleagues, even among top union officials, ever felt close to Jack Jones. That was part of his mystique and perhaps even his attraction. Outstanding leadership is always a lonely role and Jones maintained that carapace as a careful trademark. Yet he could also be extremely friendly, helpful, if not immediately sympathetic. Though rarely generous in praise he was always ready to recognise genuine talent. All these characteristics blended to make him one of the most formidable and outstanding of all post-war trade union leaders. Yet Morris retains one vignette which may or may not conflict with this image of Jones the hard man. It was Bill Morris's very first executive meeting at the union's then headquarters in Smith Square, Westminster. All thirty-nine members of the executive broke for lunch, most of them moving across to a nearby Lyons café house, close to Transport House, the union HQ, for a buffet lunch. In the queue immediately behind newcomer Morris was the general secretary, Jack Jones. As Morris chose his lunch and queued to pay a voice from behind suddenly called out, 'Have this lunch on me.' So his first executive meeting became a vivid memory of the union's boss buying the novice his lunch. Yet, as Morris reflects, 'It didn't bring us any closer.'

Not long after this experience Morris put his foot on the first rung of the ladder with his appointment in 1973, aged thirty-five, as a full-time official of the TGWU. The General Executive Council took up the recommendation from Brian Mathers, the Midlands region secretary, to appoint him as district official for the Nottingham and Derby area. Mathers was the principal trade union power in the region and anxious to break with convention by making the appointment of the union's first black full-time official. Mathers was also a man of the Left who recognised the political potential in such a historic step coming five years after the Enoch Powell event. So Mathers's influence carried weight with the union's executive council. Regional secretaries have no individual power to appoint – but their support and recommendation are important.

The work of a district organiser primarily involves day-to-day contact with all kinds of shop-floor problems, a good personal rapport with members and twenty-four-hours-a-day accessibility. Another responsibility is to recruit new members for the union, always an effective barometer for a successful official. Morris's portfolio was a hard-working schedule which included a range of quite different industries from the food trade, textiles, engineering to local authorities across the counties of Nottinghamshire and Derbyshire, much of which embraced public transport, mainly buses. To add to his workload Morris had, at first, to commute daily between Birmingham and Nottingham until he was able to find a new home in Nottingham. However, once more there was a whiff of racial prejudice when Morris used an agency to arrange to purchase a house in Nottingham but was turned down by the agency. The evidence pointed to discrimination. In the end a house was purchased with a mortgage organised and financed by the union. Being married with teenagers, the move from Birmingham to Nottingham inevitably involved a considerable disruption to the family's life. But they all settled in quite quickly and Bill was well received by his union colleagues in Nottingham. Within a couple of weeks of starting work in Nottingham he took charge of a strike that was organised at a local factory demanding union recognition. Morris enjoyed his three years in the Nottingham area. He found the whole experience an immensely valuable learning curve. It enabled him to prove his ability as a full-time official and after his three-year spell he succeeded well enough to win Brian Mathers's confidence to promote him to the higher role of district secretary at the TGWU office in Northampton. One of the first to congratulate him was George Wright, his original mentor.

Of course his move to Northampton brought an entirely different and expanded range of industries covering important new elements such as the local brewing industry. It also included the Ford car plant at Daventry and the large national headquarters of the Rugby Cement Company as well as some of his former trade sites like food and local authorities. The Morris family moved house again and with union help settled down in Northampton for another three-year stint. It was also an important time for them. Morris's two sons were growing up and reaching the end of their secondary school years. Both boys were either involved with or preparing to take their A-level examinations. It was altogether a testing time for him and Minetta who took a job in a local hospital. But the family were happily settled and liked their spell in the Northampton area. From there both the Morris boys eventually graduated to university – one going to Dundee and the other to Bradford. This in itself contains an interesting reflection on how Bill Morris overcame another aspect of racial prejudice. Both sons had started their schooling in Birmingham at local primary schools but one of the boys ran into some difficulties at his first school. When Morris looked into the problem he was told by the boy's teacher: 'The problem is that your son is educationally sub-normal.' Morris could have reacted, justifiably, with visible anger. Instead he simply removed the boys to another school. He achieved this with an extraordinary piece of personal enterprise. At the time the Morris family lived at number 124 Putney Street in Handsworth. On the opposite side of Putney Street at number 105 was a house for sale. It had the additional advantage of being in the catchment area for a different primary school from the house at number 124. So Morris sold number 124 and moved across to number 105 in the middle of one night with the help of their local friends in what was literally a midnight move organised and carried out by themselves; all to enable Bill to move his boys to a more friendly and less discriminatory school. He tells the story now with a degree of pride as he reflects on his sons' academic achievements in subsequent years – but also to emphasise his attitude towards expressions of racial bias: shrug your shoulders and get on with your job.

For Bill Morris himself the Northampton job was an important part of his overall experience and learning curve. He was in charge of the area and saw it as an opportunity to demonstrate his own ideas of how to improve the effectiveness of the union. He modernised the Northampton headquarters which had become somewhat shabby; he transformed relations between head office and the membership by introducing more direct contact between full-time officials and the shop floor, and generally injected a new dynamic to the role of the District Office. It is also worth recalling that 1976, when he started in Northampton, was an especially difficult period in British industrial relations. The national economy was in deep crisis and the trade unions had reached a critical deal with the Wilson Labour government that had negotiated a highly controversial Social Contract involving wage restraint based on a £6 limit for all pay rises. By definition that made the job of all trade union negotiations far more difficult. It left very little room for manoeuvre and his experiences at Northampton left a lasting impression on Morris concerning the problems inherent in any form of wage restraint. Moreover, it was particularly difficult for every full-time official of the TGWU since their leader, Jack Jones, had been the principal architect of the Social Contract deal with the Wilson government in the summer of 1975. This inevitably meant that T&G officials across the country felt an additional pressure on them in the way they handled their wage negotiations; and again, in Morris's case as the first and still the only black officer in the union, there was always that touch of extra pressure. Yet Morris handled his Northampton assignment with notable success. He was able to negotiate pay rises, sometimes even in excess of the £6 limit – which was not a comfortable experience for him. There was also some tension among various rank and file groups in the district at their first experience of a black area secretary. One of the union's national officers at that time was Peter Evans, who remembers going to Northampton to help Morris with a particularly complex negotiation with the Rugby Cement Company. The local workforce, which happened to be wholly white, had become deeply restive against their hostile management. There was also a history of tension between some of the active T&G members at Rugby Cement and their trade union officials. Inevitably an undercurrent of racial prejudice was something Morris had to deal with. Peter Evans remembers how well Morris handled this difficult and sensitive situation. 'He did it with great skill,' Evans recalls. 'There were no dramatics, he never allowed himself to be distracted by any racialist comment or undertones. Frankly, as a newcomer in that official role I think he did his job with remarkable skill.' Evans was, and remains, a shrewd and experienced observer and his report back to Jack Jones clearly carried weight. Morris's status grew with his experience. One manifestation of this was the reputation he established in the locality for the Transport Union. During the 'Winter of Discontent' period when there was considerable unrest and demonstrations in the area, a group of local Conservative MPs approached him to sound him out as to what could be done politically to assist the union to establish better relations with local industries.

After three years running the union's affairs in Northampton, a vacancy opened for a new national officer in London to take over the passenger services group of the TGWU, one of the union's most important and demanding areas. It involved overall responsibility for all buses and coach services across the entire country. The group had a membership of more than 140,000

– almost a mini-union in its own right (the total membership of the TGWU at that time was well over one and half million). The appointment, made at national level by the union's executive, was again the first of its kind. When Morris applied for the job he was up against very strong candidates including men with far more experience in the bus and coach operations than himself. But it was Morris who was appointed by the union's Finance and General Purposes committee.

Again it came at a critical moment for the union: Jack Jones had retired in 1978, shortly before Morris left Northampton, and Moss Evans was elected to succeed him as general secretary. That in itself was a huge change at the top of what was still Britain's largest trade union. In addition the Morris appointment as a national officer of the TGWU came as Margaret Thatcher was being elected Prime Minister to lead a Conservative government pledged to reform – and weaken – the entire trade union movement. As Bill Morris ruefully now reflects: 'Nothing came easily for me – everything I do is a first. But I let other people worry about that.' Nor did he allow the racial factor to dominate his thoughts. He had by then managed to rationalise his position and had enough confidence in his own ability to dismiss racial abuse. By the time he became a national officer of the union Morris was an altogether more mature, more rounded and experienced person with the ability to brush off what had become an almost endemic, if often concealed, attitude by some even at the higher levels of the union.

4

On the National Stage

LOOKING BACK TO THE MOMENT Bill Morris came to London as the first black national officer of any British trade union, one extraordinary aspect was the absence of major coverage in the media. In fact it went largely unreported. There were no front-page stories about a potential and unusual new 'star'; no exclusive interviews with the first black national trade union figure. A large part of this was due to Bill Morris himself. He decided quite firmly against seeking publicity and rejected several requests to be interviewed. Perhaps, once again, it was the old aspect of self-confidence; possibly even the ever-present awareness that for him to seek, or respond to the temptation of, publicity might tend to aggravate racial resentment. Morris himself looks back at that moment and explains that he simply wanted to 'get on with the job I was appointed to do' and 'let events rather than words tell the story'. Perhaps that is a reflective rationalisation entirely in character with this essentially shy man; a man who has always preferred to remain carefully guarded against intrusiveness, ever anxious to protect his inner feelings.

Of course 1979 was a busy year for industrial, political and most of all trade union news; it was the year that opened with the 'Winter of Discontent' and was finally crowned, if that is the word, with Mrs Thatcher's victory in the general election of May 1979. The appointment of a black official to the hierarchy of a trade union was small drama compared with what was happening in the wider political and industrial world. Indeed as far as the trade unions were concerned the reporting of their activities became increasingly dominated by varying accounts of trade unionism in retreat or by some key unions, like the steelworkers, being drawn into the first major strike of the Thatcher era.

Media attention alongside the new political agenda ensured that the role and indeed the very purpose of trade unionism came under the microscope in a manner unmatched in the post-war years. From the beginning of the Thatcher period it was already clear that her victory was going to mark a turning point in the power, influence and functioning of the trade unions, even though the first wave of anti-union legislation was still to come. In that sense it is not surprising that there was less than expected press attention to Bill Morris's arrival in London. Media rationale was almost certainly grounded on a simple reasoning: why bother with a still little-known trade union figure like Bill Morris even if he is black, when the future of trade unionism itself was now in the balance. By that token the general climate of the moment suited Morris's quiet landing.

Yet that was not how his appointment was viewed inside the Transport and General Workers Union which, despite the emergence of Margaret Thatcher, was still regarded as a power in the land, not least by its own senior officers. So, let us be clear about one thing – his arrival at Transport House in London's Smith Square, then the headquarters of the TGWU, was received with mixed feelings inside that building. There were those who welcomed Bill Morris with genuine warmth – delighted at the appointment of a black national officer, proud of the fact that it was the TGWU that had led the field in making the Morris appointment. There were others who guardedly reserved judgement. And there was also a significant minority who, mostly in silence, felt that it had been a mistake in the first place. Such views never openly manifested themselves in racial terms, but rather in questioning the wisdom and timing of the union's executive council. These doubters wanted to know whether Morris had been appointed on grounds of genuine ability or, as some of them suspected or preferred to believe, because the union's leadership wanted to demonstrate an example of positive discrimination in favour of a black person. There were also those who argued that the timing was inopportune coming at a moment when the trade union movement faced its greatest test since the end of the Second World War. It is impossible to know the precise truth about all the motivations surrounding Bill Morris's historic appointment in 1979. Yet for him it made little difference. He had already learned to develop the strength to turn his mind away from such prejudice. It may not have been easy but he was comforted, delighted and proud to have achieved a special moment for himself and for the union. Bill Morris's principal concern was: he had been appointed a national officer of the TGWU and he now faced new and demanding challenges. He set about moving the family home from Northampton to a house in Hemel Hempstead, a small town on the northern edge of London, the house in which he remained until his retirement from general secretaryship.

The passenger services trade group of the TGWU was a very important sector of a union that Jack Jones had turned into an organisation of over two million members by the time he retired in 1978 handing over to Moss Evans. The trade group consisted mainly of bus drivers and conductors, garage crews, coach drivers and some maintenance workers, totalling a membership of over 140,000 – a substantial slice of which was in London buses with a membership of 24,000. Morris had not been favourite to win the national officer's job. The two main candidates, Cliff Twort and Charlie Young, were both experienced London busmen, and both had strong support among London bus crews – and on a national level. Twort, who eventually was to succeed Morris in his role, and Young were convinced that one of them would get the job, and when the Finance and General Purposes Committee opted for Morris the appointment produced shock waves across the trade group. This was not simply because Morris was black but still more controversially, because he had no previous experience of bus work. His shop-floor experience was in engineering – in plants where buses were made, not driven. While it was true that he had been responsible for public transport systems – chiefly buses – as head of the union's Northampton office, that was not seen, by some of his critics, as sufficient justification to appoint him as national officer for the union's nationwide bus transport section. Moreover the London busmen in particular were a difficult group for any national official to handle. They had a long tradition as tough bargainers. They were men (and at that time they were mainly men) with great pride in their trade both as skilled drivers and as workers in a key area of public service. The busmen had their own history and indeed their own culture with a reputation for challenging the union's leadership when they felt necessary – as even Ernest Bevin had found during the 1937 London bus strike in which the London busmen's unofficial leadership gave the redoubtable Bevin a very rough time. So it was no easy task for Morris to win over the support, still less the affection, of this trade group.

He set about the task with characteristic diligence and candour. 'I knew it wouldn't be an easy road but I made it my job to get around all the bus depots and talk to the branches. It was also the beginning of a difficult period for bus services. Things were changing rapidly; public services were being privatised (part of Margaret

Thatcher's policy) and it was also a period when conductors were being replaced by multi-purpose drivers
who were expected to collect fares as well as drive their
buses. This caused a lot of tension across the trade – in
an area where tradition had a powerful hold.'

Morris's main problem was to break through this curtain of tradition and handle a situation in which change
had become unavoidable throughout the bus industry
and staff cuts were frequent as the traditional role of the
conductor began to disappear. Much of this was also
the result of rapidly changing social habits. With the
vast increase in car ownership among commuters in the
sixties there were fewer people using buses as a routine
way of getting to work and back. Services were reduced
and modified on all routes – all of which led to further
staffing cuts. There was an additional factor which may,
or may not, have helped Morris depending on local circumstances: a new drive to recruit younger busmen was
developed as older more traditional hands retired, and
this tended to include the recruitment of a substantial
number of immigrant workers. Indeed the recruitment
of immigrant bus crews started as early as the 1960s
under a Conservative government. By the time Bill Morris took over as national secretary for the group the flow
of immigrant workers into bus services was increasingly
marked. Indeed the awareness of this had probably been
an influencing factor in his appointment. For Morris in
particular there were both positive and negative aspects
in this process of a changing culture.

One of his memorable campaigns was what he

describes as the 'can't pay don't pay' protest against the removal of bus conductors. He organised a national protest against the abolition of bus conductors which called on bus passengers to refuse to pay fares on routes that were either about to be turned into driver-only services or had already been switched. In effect Morris sought to harness the ordinary working passenger alongside the union's fight to retain conductors. But the campaign was only moderately successful and hit the buffers when some conductors began to put passengers off their buses when they refused to pay fares. That setback upset Morris because it brought protests from conductor members of his trade group and in effect set them against passengers and vice versa. There were no easy solutions to this problem. Time and new technology was on the side of change. Eventually the role of the traditional conductor was phased out across all bus services and, however reluctantly, finally and doggedly accepted by the public, though to this day there remains a public murmur of discontent at the absence of conductors on buses.

Even so Morris won a great deal of support for his bargaining skills not only in his fight to improve bus workers' pay and conditions but, still more difficult, to help cushion the impact of many of the social, cultural and work changes then sweeping across the public transport industry. No doubt his major achievement as national secretary for the union's passenger services was to negotiate a thirty-eight-hour working week first for London bus crews and then for all bus workers across the country. He prided himself on being a good negotiator – 'tough but fair' is his own description – a reputation that he had in fact established both among his members and many employers. It lifted Bill Morris's profile within the union as a whole and certainly contributed to what was to follow.

The watershed year was 1985; after seven years in his role as general secretary Moss Evans was forced to retire early because of serious illness and his successor was the union's national organiser, Ron Todd, a former shop-floor worker at the huge Ford car plant in Dagenham. It was also the year of the miners' strike, the most bitter industrial dispute of the post-war years, a strike that lasted for a year and ultimately involved most of the trade unions in a fierce battle with the Thatcher government. In fact it was a year of industrial fury without parallel since the end of the Second World War. Such was Todd's inheritance.

It is generally recognised that no previous TGWU general secretary had a more difficult period in office than Ron Todd. No previous leader of the union had to face such a combination of political, industrial and social turmoil as well as challenge to the very existence and function of trade unions, perhaps only comparable with the kind of hostile climate in which Ernest Bevin battled when he formed the TGWU in the 1920s. Moreover Todd himself had to overcome an unprecedented challenge from within the union after he had been elected. This came from his principal opponent in the election campaign, George Wright, then the TGWU regional secretary for South Wales. Wright, who had campaigned on a centre-right political and industrial programme, had considerable support across most other regions against Todd's left-wing agenda. But Todd won the ballot by a clear margin only to be challenged by Wright who claimed that there had been ballot irregularities in some branches. An inquiry rejected these allegations but, true to character, Todd insisted on a second ballot for the union's top post. He refused to take up the role without the support of a clear democratic mandate from the membership. He demanded a second ballot despite being urged to ignore Wright's challenge. So a second ballot was held which Todd won with an increased majority. It was a unique triumph for the new general secretary of the TGWU and established his authority in a manner no one seriously could question. For Bill Morris the outcome of the Todd v. Wright election was to become the real turning point in his career. In retrospect it can be seen as the decisive event leading to the opening of the door enabling Morris eventually to take the top post.

Of course the defeat of George Wright might seem on face value to have been a disappointment to Morris since here was the man who had pioneered his rise from the shop floor. Indeed the man who, effectively, had set him on the path to national office. It was the same George Wright who went back to Morris's earliest days in Birmingham. There was a vast irony in what happened next, because it was Ron Todd then who took

Morris under his wing and it was Todd above anyone who saw in Morris a historic potential for the TGWU – a possible future general secretary who also happened to be a black immigrant.

This, to be sure, was also in line with Todd's own political instincts. As a man of the left he had long supported the 'Cousins revolution' of the mid-fifties which had transformed the union. He backed Cousins's campaign for nuclear disarmament and the left-wing political agenda set out during Cousins's leadership of the TGWU. He equally fervently supported Cousins's fight against racial discrimination. Todd never made any pretences about wanting to be a leader in the Cousins mould – despite the severe problems involved in leading any trade union at that time, when the Thatcher social revolution was reaching its peak with her campaign against trade unionism. One of Ron Todd's special interests was to involve himself as an active participant in the campaign against apartheid in South Africa and in doing so he found a platform from which to oppose the Thatcher government's complicity in the maintenance of, or at best a failure to clearly oppose, the racialist apartheid regime in that country. Along with his union Todd played a prominent part in a TUC programme that provided significant aid to the anti-apartheid movement both inside South Africa and elsewhere. It was therefore no great surprise to find Todd keenly supporting the development and promotion of Bill Morris – though he did so quietly and with care, always conscious of the tensions within his own union. Even so Todd was able to help and encourage Morris's development as a national officer and when the opportunity arose for a further significant development in Morris's career it was Todd who provided the crucial bridge. That moment came when Morris was encouraged to take the decisive step towards leadership of the TGWU – by accepting to be nominated for the vacancy of deputy general secretary, the number two slot in the hierarchy.

The process of selecting and appointing a new deputy general secretary was an institutionalised arrangement governed by the union's rule book. By tradition nominations were made and sifted and a shortlist selected by the Finance and General Purposes Committee – which was the powerful inner cabinet group of the union and custodian both of its policy and rule book. The eleven members of this committee were, at that time, politically weighted to the Right with some seven of its members opposed to people like Bill Morris on political if not racial grounds. There was one representative from each of the union's eleven regions – the section of the union where Morris's support was weakest given the attitude of most regional secretaries, all powerful figures within their own domain. Most of them regarded Morris as a candidate being pushed by the Left inside the union and they were certainly not prepared to give a black candidate the benefit of the doubt.

The crucial process that eventually led to Bill Morris's appointment as deputy general secretary began at ten a.m. on the morning of Friday, 13 September 1985 when the eleven members of the Finance and General Purposes Committee met at the union's headquarters, which was still at its old citadel in Transport House, Smith Square.

Both the TGWU general secretary Ron Todd and his then deputy Alex Kitson were ex-officio members of this top committee and were present at the meeting, though they did not technically have a vote. Ray Collins, the union's administrative officer, effectively the general secretary's chief lieutenant was also present – again in an ex-officio capacity. Collins witnessed an extraordinary process as the committee discussed a list of thirteen candidates which included two regional secretaries, five national secretaries of trade groups, the union's legal secretary, three national officers, one lay member and an assistant general secretary, Larry Smith, who was number three in the pecking order after the general secretary and his deputy. Smith was in fact a strong contender supported by the right wing. If not the favourite he was regarded as the strongest candidate. Bill Morris, a national secretary, was one of the thirteen. He was aware that the dice was loaded against him. The whole process was also further complicated by the F&GP Committee being called on to shortlist candidates for two jobs – the deputy general secretary and a new assistant general secretary, number three in the pecking order. Some of the thirteen contestants had thrown their hat into the ring for both jobs – including Morris along with five others.

The crunch came when the F&GP Committee

decided not to shortlist Morris for either. The five names chosen to go to the final stage, which was a session before the full General Executive Council, the ultimate ruling authority, were: the legal secretary Albert C. Blyghton; the assistant general secretary Larry Smith; two regional secretaries, Joe Mills and Mel Snow and a national officer, Fred J. Howell. Collins was absent for the afternoon session when the F&GP completed its shortlist. He learned about it later from Ron Todd who was fuming with indignation – not least because he saw it as a personal snub since the F&GP were quite aware that Todd favoured Morris's candidature.

That night Ron Todd phoned Bill Morris to explain what had happened and told him: 'I'm not having it, Bill.' He made it clear to Bill Morris that he would go to the General Executive meeting the following Monday and argue that the F&GP had failed in its responsibilities and that the Executive could and should now use its authority to change the process – as was within their power, Todd argued. Todd also instructed Collins to make the necessary arrangements to enable all thirteen original candidates to present their own case before the full Executive, then under the chairmanship of Walter Greendale, a former Hull dockworker. It was not so much that Todd was bending the rule book, the union's bible, but rather that he was re-stating the responsibilities that lay in the hands of the full Executive. Even so the effect of Todd's intervention was clearly to advocate that the Executive should overturn the F&GP decision. On the morning of Monday, 16 September, before the

Executive assembled, Ron Todd delayed the opening session to enable him to speak to the five men who had been shortlisted as they waited to be called before the General Executive. He made it quite clear that his purpose was to determine a fair decision was reached in making both appointments – for the deputy general secretary, the key role as his number two, as well as the appointment of a new assistant general secretary. He insisted on all thirteen candidates returning to present their case individually before the full Executive. There was no doubting the irritation, even the anger, of the five who had been previously shortlisted by the F&GP – notably Larry Smith who plainly felt he had been cornered and who finally pulled out of the contest.

Todd's insistence that the whole procedure be reopened at the Monday meeting of the full General Executive Council was without question a dramatic intervention which was to produce an equally dramatic outcome. There is no recorded parallel for such a move in such critical circumstances. The union's general secretary had never disguised his desire that the TGWU should set a new pattern in race relations by appointing Bill Morris to a senior role; nor had he disguised his contempt and anger for what had happened the previous Friday when Morris had been deliberately 'frozen out'. But he also respected the union's rule book and his objective was to restore fairness in appointing a new number two without flouting the rules of the union. His shrewd diplomacy along with his clear moral purpose combined to produce this most extraordinary turnaround in the entire process of Morris's appointment.

At the crucial meeting of the full thirty-eight-member General Executive that Monday morning Todd (an ex-officio member of the Executive along with his then deputy Alex Kitson, Ray Collins and Harry Timpson, the financial secretary) set the tone by restating his purpose in overturning the F&GP shortlisting.

Yet his intervention was not delivered in any arrogant, dictatorial style. There was no table-thumping, though there was a visible display of his inner anger. Nor did he specify his personal preference for Bill Morris. He was too experienced, too wily a man to adopt that stance – which, in any event, might have been counter-productive. In the past tradition of the union's leadership – with men like Ernest Bevin – that might have been the case. But not with Todd. It was not his style. He argued his case with firm persuasiveness, placing great emphasis on his belief that the moment had arrived for the TGWU to take a lead in appointing someone whom he recognised might well excite controversy but who nonetheless was, in his opinion, by far the best candidate for the job. The time had come, Todd argued, for the union to set an example to the whole Labour Movement and take a much broader look at the future leadership of the union and its potential.

There then followed individual submissions by all the candidates on the original list with each contribution tape-recorded for the record. Two dropped out, the lay member J. Court and a national officer W. Nortcliffe, which left eleven individual submissions. By common consent the majority agreed that the submission by Bill Morris was one of the most outstanding of all. The result was a complete reversal of the decision previously taken and Morris was added to a shortlist of five, which embraced both the deputy general secretaryship and the assistant general secretaryship. The meeting was then adjourned with a final decision left for the following day. After further brief submissions and a few questions to each, the vote was taken. Minute No. 714 of Tuesday, 17 September 1985 records as follows: 'Resolved: That brother W.M. Morris (national secretary of the passenger services group) be appointed to the position of deputy general secretary at the salary and subject to the conditions associated with the position.' And that was that. Ray Collins was at that meeting and says that Bill Morris made by far the best submission and 'was the most impressive candidate'. It was indeed a watershed for the union as well as for the entire British trade union movement. And it had been established largely because of the convictions of one man, the leader of the TGWU Ron Todd, in his visionary determination to defy the critics and opposition within his own union and demonstrate that the time had come to set an example and precedent for others to follow if they so wished. For Todd himself most important of all it had shown that his union, the TGWU, with all its history and traditions was still capable of setting the pace in a vital moral, social and political context. History had been made by both men – Bill Morris, with thanks to Ron Todd.

It is worth pausing for a moment here to evaluate the importance, and the courage, of Todd's initiative leading to Morris's appointment. In a way both men – Todd and Morris – had been inspired by the revolution which Frank Cousins had brought to the TGWU. In their different ways they were both products of that transformation in the mid-fifties. But of course thirty years on from that period the scene had shifted dramatically. The Thatcher ethos was itself a manifestation of this change. There was less tolerance of trade unions, a sharper sense of personal searching – some would call it selfishness – had entered the social climate, there was a brittleness to social relationships which to a large extent had worn away the post-war years of greater national cohesion. It has also to be said that there was evidence of growing resentment against the widespread increase in immigration and an assumption, however irrational, that old British customs had begun to wear thin. It would be an exaggeration to suggest that all these perceptions had become focused in Ron Todd's mind when he sought to encourage Bill Morris as his potential successor. Yet the evidence available does suggest that these thoughts were there and that Todd's idealism persuaded him that it was within his capacity to set an example in an attempt to challenge many of the unattractive aspects of British society that were manifest in the 1980s. It might also be recalled that at the time of Morris's appointment in 1985 Margaret Thatcher had just completed her conquest of the miners after their year-long bitter strike.

There is certainly no evidence that the occasion of

Bill Morris's appointment had any parallel in the traditional culture of the TGWU which was then still the largest trade union in the land and still holding a significant political influence – albeit with a declining membership.

Bill Morris took up his office as deputy general secretary in June 1986 after the retirement of Alex Kitson. It was quite a long period of patient expectation as he waited in the corridors of the union's hierarchy. He was aware of unpleasant whisperings about the role played by Ron Todd in his appointment – something recalled to this day – but he took all that in his stride. By then he was experienced enough in the marketplace of trade union gossip and intrigue to pick up the threads of distaste and simply ignore them. Such resentments, racial or otherwise, had long since stopped worrying him – at least on the surface. He was accustomed to that norm and he knew that he would have to face far tougher challenges in the future. But he could also comfort himself with the recognition that he was the first black person to reach the number two spot in any British trade union; that he was also the first who had risen from being a lay member of the union's General Executive Committee to receive such an appointment. He was also aware that the doorway to the top had now been opened even if the key was not yet to hand.

How did it happen? The brutally frank answer is: Ron Todd. It is probable if not certain that Morris would not have been appointed to that pivotal role but for Todd's intervention. It is also beyond reasonable doubt that

Todd was convinced, correctly or otherwise, that it had been racial discrimination which had motivated the original decision by the union's senior sub-committee, its F&GP, in excluding Morris from the shortlist. It was Todd's stunning courage in challenging all this which finally turned the moment in Morris's favour. Morris himself does not question this assessment. In his own words he told the author: 'Ron Todd showed amazing courage in challenging the authority of the rule book, or at least its interpretation by the F&GP, in killing the original shortlist. Quite frankly I cannot think of any previous general secretary, apart from Frank Cousins, who would have had the courage and the determined will to do that.'

It was indeed a defining moment for Bill Morris and the TGWU and for the British trade union movement. When Morris was informed that he had been selected he took it quietly and calmly. On that Tuesday evening in September 1985 he went back to Minetta at their Hemel Hempstead home to give her the news. They embraced each other and together, in silence, shared moments of tears. No words were exchanged, none were needed.

5

Number Two in the Union

BILL MORRIS TOOK OFFICE as the deputy general secretary of the Transport and General Workers Union at the beginning of June 1986, almost eight months after his actual appointment as number two to Ron Todd. It was an impatient, difficult waiting period. It was also coupled briefly with continuing to run his old job as national secretary for passenger services group until a successor was appointed. Then he started to pick up the threads in his demanding new role as Ron Todd's deputy. It was not an easy atmosphere. Morris was aware that he would have to carve out a role for himself without much positive help from his colleagues at national level. He knew that he had few close allies apart from the general secretary. He also knew that those who had tried to curb his advance would not yield in their resistance and criticism. At the same time he recognised that this was not a simple, straightforward matter of Left v. Right in the normal political sense. Rather it consisted

of a complex web of personal rivalries and tribal prejudices which certainly embraced racial attitudes. It
was also linked to a long history of regional tensions
within this powerful national institution. The assumption, often and easily made, that socialists and trade
unionists can usually find an inner ethical strength to
rise above such squalid behaviour is, to be sure, a sad
naivety. Life is never that simple in the climb to the top
of any pyramid. Bill Morris was compelled to come to
terms with cruel reality and he did. He quickly discovered that various prominent members of the traditional
Left in the union, including members of the Communist
Party, had opposed his appointment as deputy general
secretary on the grounds that 'the union's membership
were not yet ready to vote for a black leader.' That, of
course, was an old saw used by those who could think
of no better argument to excuse their support for an
otherwise insupportable case. Indeed it was precisely
this kind of hypocritical reasoning that had given Ron
Todd so much frustration and trouble when he moved
in to overrule the opposition to Morris's appointment.
For Todd, a man of the Left deeply motivated to assist
greater racial equality, it had been a painful experience
to hear his fellow trade unionists put forward what
he firmly believed were fallacious arguments. Yet this
was a problem Todd had to contend with for the rest
of his general secretaryship, especially when it became
increasingly evident that he wanted Bill Morris as his
successor. The original grouping of Morris's opponents
on the F&GP Committee never forgave Todd for backing

Morris, nor did numerous others who occupied senior national posts in the TGWU. The conspiracy to weaken Morris and, as some certainly had as their objective, to actually have him removed from his post as Todd's deputy remained a persistent shadow hanging over the newly promoted deputy general secretary. This internal revolt against Bill Morris never subsided. It continued in various forms and at different levels within the union throughout his period as deputy general secretary and indeed moved over into his first spell as Todd's successor. Factions on the Right and the Left were together frequently involved in numerous conspiracies. In that sense it might be argued that Morris was never entirely free from such antagonistic pressures for the whole of his tenure at the top of the TGWU, right up to the closing stages of his reign as general secretary, although after his convincing re-election to the post in the midnineties he was then in an immeasurably stronger position through to retirement. Yet the shadow of earlier prejudice never fully disappeared.

Of course while he remained at the helm Ron Todd was aware of this antipathy toward his deputy. Indeed he, too, needed allies to protect his own back since he alienated some of his old support when he made it clear that he wanted Morris as his deputy. Yet Todd was more experienced than his new deputy in handling these conspiracies. To begin with, he was secure in his role and he was white. His long career from the days as a shop steward in the then massive Ford car plant in Dagenham had shaped a shrewd toughness towards difficult opponents not only among Ford management, but equally with trade union mates who could sometimes be more awkward to handle than even his employers. Todd's generosity of spirit and his sensitive humanity helped disguise this inner toughness. Yet it was there when required.

Todd had also built up strong support from left-wing leaders in other unions – a notable ally was Rodney Bickerstaffe, general secretary of UNISON, the main public service union. He also sustained a highly popular reputation across the trade union movement and was well equipped to engage the plotters when required. Indeed his opponents often underestimated his skill, courage and determination to fight prejudice wherever it emerged – from the Right, the Left or as occurred at a later stage, even from some leading figures in the Labour Party.

Nonetheless Bill Morris's years as deputy general secretary were never easy. The internal struggle for power inside the General Executive Council and among some national officials continued to cause him problems and at times probably harmed the effectiveness of the union itself. A number of national officer appointments were frequently disputed – generally because of political rivalries. One example of this was the appointment of an assistant general secretary, a role designated as a 'number three' in the pecking order. This post was eventually given to Eddie Haigh who had been leader of a textile union which had merged with the TGWU. Haigh then found himself thrown into the internal conflicts of the TGWU as a possible opponent against Bill Morris. And although Haigh never actually competed against Morris in a union election, the hostility between them led to a difficult relationship eventually resolved when Haigh took early retirement. It also needs to be remembered that these internal battles were hammering away on Ron Todd's door at the very same time that Margaret Thatcher was in full flow conducting her crusade to weaken trade union influence across the entire national scene.

In this respect a crucial test was to come with the Prime Minister's introduction of new legislation to curb trade union independence and indeed their central powerbase. She and her ministers, especially her new employment secretary Norman Tebbitt, produced a further Bill (the 1988 Employment Act) which was designed to strengthen and reinforce a previous Act of 1984. The principal objective of this new legislation was to place a legal obligation on all trade unions to conduct secret membership ballots for all senior national officials. Where the top officers had previously been appointed by their own union executives, or even via internal voting systems, the new legislation required the removal of these internal systems to be replaced by ballots of all individual union members, across the board. Effectively it was a form of general election for trade union leaders. This of course included posts such as deputy and/or assistant general secretaryship roles as well as the top job. The thrust of this legislation removed an important power from the remit of internal union committees – such as the F&GP Committee of the TGWU – a power they had long enjoyed. Norman Tebbitt justified the new legislation by describing it as 'handing power back to trade union members'. To be sure, technically there was nothing undemocratic about this – except it inevitably invited an even wider development of tribal venom to develop within some trade unions. Nor is there anything particularly new in recognising that mass balloting, by definition, offers a temptation to corrupt practices – whether in trade unions, tennis clubs or any other organisations. Corruption could – and sometimes did – occur in such circumstances as it has (and still does) with postal voting even in general elections for a new government. It was certainly an additional problem which Morris had to face when his term as deputy general secretary came up for renewal in an open election.

The shadow of alleged ballot-rigging loomed when Todd himself was elected as general secretary which was well before the Thatcher/Tebbitt legislation. At that time the TGWU had always reserved just one senior post for a national ballot of all its members – the general secretary's job. The rest of appointments, by tradition, were decided by the system of internal appointment. Remembering what had happened during his election for general secretary Todd was only too aware of the problems that could arise when Bill Morris had to face a test of the membership vote. This was much in his mind when that moment occurred in 1990.

Meanwhile, the most significant shift in Morris's new responsibilities was moving from having had a specific remit in a single trade group to one of helping the general secretary to look after the broad interests of *all* the membership, whatever their trade, differing regional problems or sectional interests. Morris recognised that this inescapably would bring him into conflict with various regional secretaries who were known to have been opposed to his appointment. They were also men deeply rooted in their local industrial and political cultures and often seen as emperors in their own domain. Morris and his supporters across the regions knew this and prepared themselves to fight the prejudice. One of Morris's first moves was to tour every one of the union's regions which stretched across the whole of the British Isles. There were eleven separate regional authorities within the TGWU covering Wales, Scotland and Ireland as well as across England. And while he no longer had responsibility for day-to-day negotiations on pay and working conditions in any specific group he was entitled to range across the spectrum and help develop union strategy. Morris also had a responsibility for local appointments and for the overall financial structure of the TGWU on which he was deputed to advise the general secretary – a factor which was to become of crucial significance when later he would assume that position. Above all he also had a key role in helping to stop the decline in membership and to consider whether the union's recruiting system was adequate to the increasingly difficult task of winning new members. In this context one of his most considerable successes came in 1987 when the union launched a campaign called Link-up on behalf of the country's six million temporary and part-time workers, most of whom were women. Against a background of falling membership overall this was a most encouraging and successful campaign. It struck a chord across all sections of working people – especially younger workers in new industries who were incensed at the bleak attitude adopted by numerous employers in denying temporary workers many of the basic rights of normal working life. These included such issues as: parallel pay and conditions alongside permanent employees, protection against unfair dismissal, job-training opportunities and health and safety protection. Most of all there was a near total absence of any recognition of family responsibilities for young married couples. The fight for equal rights took off with a substantial national campaign which was assisted by support from the then Labour Party leader Neil Kinnock who shared union platforms with Bill Morris. Kinnock himself was a member of the TGWU. This campaign was one of Morris's most significant achievements during his period as deputy general secretary.

In addition, Morris's remit included responsibility for the union's four major transport sectors, as well as the car industry, energy resources, and the special section dealing with white-collar workers. He was charged with helping to facilitate educational opportunities within the union – similar to those he himself had enjoyed as a young shop steward in Birmingham. And it fell to the deputy general secretary to develop a campaign to recruit more women workers and to ensure they were given union assistance in seeking to achieve equal status and opportunities at work. Not surprisingly Morris was always conscious of his own experiences as a young worker, reflecting on what George Wright had done to help him develop and advance. The workload was demanding but Morris carried it out with skill, tact and tenacity which both surprised and perhaps even brought reluctant regard from his critics. His reputation as an effective deputy to Todd was notably strengthened. Even his detractors were compelled to recognise that he was now an accepted part of the union's hierarchy. Despite all that had gone before, including residual disapproval, Bill Morris, through hard work and sheer ability, succeeded in building up an impressive following along with a reputation for efficient administration. One event in particular helped to establish his credentials – a fight against the Thatcher government's proposal to abolish the National Dock Labour Scheme. This was a system which guaranteed dockworkers employment in what previously was a desperately casual industry. Before the Second World War dockers across the nation's ports were treated like virtual slave labour. There was no work security and port employers traded on a casual labour force held in place by the fear of unemployment. During the Second World War Ernest Bevin, then operating as Churchill's Minister of Labour, with sweeping new powers had set up the National Dock Labour Scheme which gave work guarantees to all dockers. It was a treasured achievement by Bevin and his union. But of course by the 1980s this was anathema to Mrs Thatcher's government and she was determined to abolish it, arguing the need for modernisation in the port industry. There was a predictable uproar from the dockers and the TGWU leadership came under immense pressure to call a national dock strike which Ron Todd, with great reluctance, resisted because it would have led the union into the Law Courts against the Thatcher government's legislation. That could have wrecked the union's finances. Todd had little option but to turn down the demand from his dockers for a national strike, which put tremendous strain on his leadership. In mid-stream he fell ill and Bill Morris stepped temporarily into his shoes. It could hardly have been a worse scenario for deputy Morris. Yet by general consent he handled a tense and at times desperate situation with exceptional care and diplomacy pending Todd's return. Even his most unforgiving critics were surprised and no doubt a touch dismayed by his success. When Todd came back after a brief absence he was confronted by angry dockers who invaded the union's headquarters threatening officials with violence. It was an ugly, critical situation for the union as a whole but especially for its leadership. In the end the dockers' resistance collapsed, albeit in the most bitter circumstances. The experience was held against Todd despite the impossible situation into which he and the union had been thrown by Thatcher's new laws. Yet, paradoxically, no parallel criticism was held against

Morris: on the contrary he was admired for his handling of the interregnum during Todd's absence. Ironically, perhaps even irrationally, it helped fortify Morris's position.

Morris was also now qualifying for appointments to outside organisations as a representative of trade union interests. Todd recommended his election to a range of bodies including the Employment Appeals Tribunal, the General Advisory Boards of the BBC and Independent Broadcasting Authority, as well as a predictable appointment to the Commission for Racial Equality on which he served for ten years. Gradually a general public image of Bill Morris was developing almost by accident – certainly not by design. It was a casual image but that was no handicap since it helped Morris's profile to rise above earlier hypocrisies, as well as the jealousies, with their shallow personal rivalries and prejudices, that had characterised so much of earlier events. An outside world slowly became more familiar with the name Bill Morris, that Transport Union chappie who was also black.

Not that this curbed his critics. Their stronghold remained principally among the TGWU's right of centre officials who continued to operate steadfastly for several years, ensuring he was kept off the General Council of the TUC despite the tradition, long established, that the union's deputy leader should be an automatic choice for the TUC's ruling council. That tradition was broken in the case of Bill Morris. For three years a right-wing opponent was consistently nominated to sit on the TUC General Council largely to keep Morris off. But he was finally nominated successfully for the General Council at the TUC's 1988 Congress. This came shortly before his re-appointment as number two to Ron Todd.

That re-appointment followed on from an achievement that was as remarkable and certainly as significant as Morris's original appointment in 1985 after the intervention by Ron Todd. It was the first time Bill Morris's role in the union was confirmed in a national ballot of the union's membership. The political as well as social significance of that result cannot be underestimated. Morris was the first TGWU senior official tested under Mrs Thatcher's new legislation demanding a full membership vote for all top trade union appointments.

Bill Morris's re-appointment as number two to Ron Todd in the 1990 election for deputy general secretary was given an overwhelming endorsement. It has to be said that the poll was low. Out of the union's total membership, at that time 1,138,093, only about one in four troubled to vote. Even so it was a crucial test of the membership's reaction to a leader who had already encountered so much racial hostility. Moreover there had been considerable publicity surrounding the contest – not least because of its relevance to the Thatcher/ Tebbit new law on trade union voting. By any measure it was a vital test of the pulse of the Labour Movement.

The candidate most rumoured to run against Bill Morris was the ardent left-wing regional secretary in

Northern Ireland, John Freeman, who had long made it clear he was opposed to Bill Morris for a range of reasons and had associated with the tribal opposition on the union's executive council. But to the surprise of many he announced he would not stand. Instead the most prominent left-wing candidate was John Atkins, a rank and file member of the union's General Executive Council. A third candidate was another rank and file member: S. Boucher. The voting took place in June 1990 closing on 22 June and the result was:

> Bill Morris: 128,657
> John Atkins: 56,865
> S. Boucher: 42,001

Of course this was an immense boost to Bill Morris; a boost for his self-confidence and self-esteem; and perhaps above all the awareness that he had overcome the long and distressing pressure of racial prejudice. Morris's victory was a clear signal throughout the union that he was now a confirmed number two to the general secretary. Still more it was a substantial signal that he was now the most probable successor to Ron Todd. It was also a highly important development for the union itself inasmuch as it had demonstrated the trade union capacity to overcome the hurdle of the Thatcher/Tebbit legislation. Bill Morris himself took the victory quite calmly and rationally. He knew it would not eliminate the prejudice or the criticism that had been ranged against him for so long.

Yet there were other things he had to contend with. At that moment of triumph he also faced a profound emotional shock and setback – the serious illness of his beloved wife Minetta, and the death soon after of his devoted mother – the two women closest to him who had played such a major influence in his life.

The two deaths hit Morris within five months of each other, spanning the end of 1989 and into 1990, at the critical time of his election campaign for re-appointment as deputy general secretary. Adding to the shock waves of these two traumatic events was the death of the family dog, Ashe, to whom both he and Minetta, and their two boys, had been devoted for fourteen years. They had named Ashe, a black Labrador, after the famed black tennis player Arthur Ashe. The blows came one on top of the other and hit him very hard indeed. The cliché 'devastated' is appropriate though still fails fully to describe his desolation in the first days of 1990 after Minetta died from breast cancer. His teenage sweetheart whom he met and married when he was nineteen and with whom he had spent thirty-three years of happy and inspired marriage suddenly dropped from his life. He still broods in silent introspection and even self-criticism about that period in his life. He is on record with a confession of personal grief during a BBC programme, *Desert Island Discs*, broadcast in 1998, by which time he had already become general secretary, the historic achievement that Minetta did not live to see. In that programme Bill Morris referred to Minetta as 'the wind beneath my wings'. That broadcast elicited a huge wave of sympathy and was reported in the national press at the time as having memorably moved a wide audience. Shortly afterwards he told the *Sunday Times* in an interview:*

'There's not a waking day that I don't think and remember. It's too important a part of your life to forget. It's like forgetting Jamaica.' He also confessed to having himself failed, at that time, to fully appreciate the severity of Minetta's illness. When she was operated on for breast cancer and appeared to recover Minetta returned to her job as a fully trained nurse. But the cancer returned and she died soon afterwards. Bill Morris still harbours a feeling of guilt about his failing to recognise the gravity of the disease. 'My regret is that I didn't make enough of those years … I wouldn't talk about it, and she wanted me to … I talked about everything else except what was important to her. We could have had some real quality days although I'm not even sure how much quality those days would have had because we would have been doing it for a reason …' Bill Morris's profound regret is that Minetta was not alive to see him elected as general secretary of the TGWU. That would have been a crowning glory for the marriage.

Soon after Minetta's death Bill Morris's mother died in Birmingham; and following her death the family dog Ashe also died. He describes the poignant moment when he returned to their home in Hemel Hempstead

---

* *The Sunday Times,* 10 September.2000

from the hospital where Minetta died in the early days of January 1990: 'I was stunned. I remember putting a few clothes into the washing machine and as I closed the machine suddenly thinking to myself "Why am I doing this – because I am now on my own."'

His private ordeals had two major influences on the pattern of his life over the next few years. He threw all his energy into his role as deputy general secretary, propelling him into a virtual non-stop work schedule. Secondly, it fortified an inner determination to do all possible to strengthen his case for succession when Ron Todd retired as general secretary of the TGWU. In that sense the grievous personal losses seemed to inject him with extra willpower and an inner strength to achieve that historic goal. Each setback appeared to fortify his resolve and his self-esteem which had consistently been tested under the trials of racial abuse. Morris's quiet enclosed dignity was his protective armour.

At the same time his political profile was also raised, partly by circumstances but equally because he wanted to broaden his role in the Labour Party and to play his part on Labour Party platforms and within the Party's policymaking structure – a role that was indeed in the tradition of the deputy general secretary of the Party's strongest affiliate union. He did not become a member of the Party's National Executive Committee, which had been the norm for the number two in the TGWU but he was elected chairman of the highly influential Conference Arrangements Committee. This was a committee of top trade union leaders whose main role was to manage the annual Party conference. Nor was its agenda confined to the conference week. Its work schedule usually began well in advance of the annual gathering of Party delegates, with its decisions determining the shape and conduct of the conference. Morris's appointment to this key role as chairman of the committee gave him unparalleled status as well as access to the Labour Party's hierarchy. Taking over in the autumn of 1990 helped to cushion the emotional upheaval of the events that had occurred in the earlier part of the year and certainly added to his growing self-confidence. An example of this was his determined rejection of pressure from many black members in the Labour Party, and from other trade unions, as well as his own for specific black sections both within the Labour Party and the TUC. Morris wouldn't have this at all. He was firmly opposed to separatist moves of this kind though he knew that such opposition could expose him to fierce criticism from many friends in the black community. Yet he stood firmly on the issue, arguing: 'I have never supported separatist black sections. I have always stood for black representation – and in all trade unions there is now a policy on race.'

In the run-up to the 1992 general election there was an increasing confidence among the trade unions that Labour could finally manage to dislodge the Conservatives who, now under John Major, had been in power since 1979. The Party leader Neil Kinnock had strong links with the trade unions and especially his own union, the TGWU. He was also a great admirer of Bill Morris with whom he frequently shared Labour Party platforms. At the same time Morris was developing his own political credentials as a firm but moderate left-wing candidate for an election that everyone knew would not be long delayed – not so much the general election of 1992 but the election for a successor to Ron Todd as future general secretary of the TGWU. Scarcely a speech made by Morris in 1990 and 1991, the year of his election to succeed Todd, came without a strong political undertone. Perhaps most significant of all was the one he delivered at the traditional left-wing rally of the *Tribune* magazine – a fringe gathering held for years halfway through Labour's conference week at which outstanding figures of the Left, notably Aneurin Bevan and Michael Foot, had pronounced on what they believed Party policy should be. Bill Morris used the *Tribune* platform during the 1990 Labour Party conference in effect to put forward a clear left-wing agenda for his own forthcoming election. He denied this at the time but it was obvious to everyone that this is what he had in mind, quite apart from his call for a socialist policy from a future Labour government he hoped would be elected at the approaching general election in 1992, the same year that Ron Todd's successor would be taking over at the TGWU.

'Some people,' he told that *Tribune* rally, 'have been trying to write off the Left in the Labour Party. They say the Left is exhausted, devoid of ideas, defeated and demoralised. As a trade unionist I would have given up long ago if I had taken such a defeatist attitude to life. I believe the democratic Left is alive and well. We have not been stamped out and we have a major role to play in the period ahead.' Then, in his peroration, came the pointer to his own future role as an aspiring leader of the TGWU – he claimed that his union had put itself at the helm of the left-wing bid to help shape future Labour Party policy. 'It is the Left which is the guardian of socialism,' he told the rally. 'It is the Left within my union who have set the agenda on every major issue.'

In previous speeches Morris had already clarified his own position on such key issues as wages policy, equal rights for women workers, taxation of the wealthy, disarmament – all traditional left-wing issues that had characterised the Transport Union leadership policy since the days of Frank Cousins. Morris now increasingly emphasised his opposition to wage restraint, or any form of incomes policy, and aligned himself alongside Todd's long-standing support for nuclear disarmament, the very issue that in earlier years Cousins had stamped on the trade union and Labour Movement as a Transport Union speciality. Yet Morris was also careful to avoid being linked with extreme leftist views. His political position was markedly left of centre; he was a radical. But he also tempered his left-wing case with reasoned balance – which sometimes encouraged his critics on the far Left to distrust his left-wing claims. Morris was always careful to tailor his radicalism to the political mood of the Labour Party, its voters as well as his own members. It was his style to offer an increasingly mature political balance as he prepared for his election to succeed Ron Todd. Yet this also added to his problems since it reinforced his left-wing critics inside the union. But now Morris realised only too well that there was an absolute requirement to be constantly on guard against the rival factions within both Left and Right groupings of the union. At times the intrigue against him continued to be based primarily on racial prejudice. Bill Morris knew his opponents would have no compunction in seeking to undermine him on the pretext of 'political opportunism' – which, in reality, was their cover phrase to mask the opposition to him on personal and of course, however much they sought to conceal it, on racialist grounds.

6

General Secretary

IT WAS ON 7 FEBRUARY 1991 when Bill Morris publicly declared his intention to seek election as general secretary of the Transport and General Workers Union. He was fifty-two years old and had established himself in the hierarchy of the union despite all obstacles thrown across his path. He had also been Ron Todd's number two in command for five years and was powerfully fortified by his re-election as deputy general secretary in a ballot of the national membership.

The process of electing a new leader of the union was of course full of procedural complexities woven into the history and tradition of the TGWU going back to Bevin's days. The outgoing general secretary, Ron Todd, was responsible for ensuring that the ballot for his succession would be conducted in absolute probity. He was especially anxious that the long story of prejudice against Bill Morris would not be allowed to corrupt the process and of course he was fully aware of the problems endemic to the nature of such a national ballot; after all he himself had been the victim of allegations of unfairness and irregularities when he had fought his first election against George Wright. So in launching the election for his succession Todd began by informing his senior executive committee, the Finance and General Purposes group, that he proposed to retire the following year when he would reach the age of sixty-five. He then instructed the committee to begin planning for the election and reminded them of the need to allow at least three months to conduct the ballot. He also made a special point of emphasising how crucial it was for the union and its reputation to ensure the election was conducted in a spirit of visible fairness, free from any accusations that might damage its credibility. The members of the union's senior committee knew exactly what Todd was referring to. No questions or comments were necessary.

These were the formalities at the opening stages of a process that would eventually bring Bill Morris to the pinnacle of his achievements. Yet there remained another year to go before he would eventually take over from Todd and it was abundantly clear that nothing was going to be simple, straightforward or easy for Morris in the interim. Even the well-advertised support he was receiving from Ron Todd carried its own boomerang effect. Morris had no illusions about the pitfalls, or to use a more appropriate metaphor, the tank traps that lay ahead.

From the very outset no one could fail to recognise

the danger signs flashing across Morris's path. Yet the biggest warning signal came at a time and from a source least expected. It emerged well before Todd announced his retirement plans and genuinely shocked even the best-informed observers. As the annual conference of the Labour Party was opening at Blackpool in late September 1990 there came an astonishing tactical gambit from, of all people, George Wright, the man who had been Morris's original mentor. Suddenly and unexpectedly Wright declared his intention to contest again for the general secretaryship.

In many ways this has to be seen as the greatest irony in the remarkable career of Bill Morris. For here was the very person who, more than anyone else, had been largely responsible for identifying Morris's potential when he was a shop-floor worker at Hardy Spicer in Birmingham and then providing the necessary help and mentorship that had started Morris on the road to the top of the union. Now Wright, the mentor, decided to make what amounted to a late comeback attempt to seize the top job from Morris's grasp. Twice defeated by Ron Todd and still resenting that failure, George Wright, the TGWU chief man for the Wales region, planned a final assault on the summit. Not only that, but he chose to announce and launch his campaign when least expected and arguably when least appropriate – well ahead of any discussion or planning by the union's hierarchy. To everyone's amazement – most of all Todd's – the Wright campaign actually opened on 29 September 1990 on the very first day of the Blackpool

Party conference. Quite plainly it had been well planned in advance by Wright's supporters and designed to outflank both Ron Todd and Bill Morris. Todd immediately launched a counter-attack first by publicly criticising Wright for jumping the gun and then writing to the Labour Party leader Neil Kinnock apologising for this unseemly 'distraction' by George Wright at the very outset of the Party conference. Todd accused his Wales region secretary of having thrown the highly controversial issue of the future general secretaryship of the TGWU, Labour's largest trade union affiliate, like a bombshell into the cauldron of Party conference week on the very first day. Inevitably George Wright's announcement overshadowed normal business.

So, why did Wright choose to play his cards this way? Was it, coming from such a senior and experienced figure, a cardinal error of judgement? Possibly. Yet from his point of view the dramatic move to leap ahead of any planned election schedule, calculated to wrongfoot both Todd and Morris, might well have proved a brilliant strategy. Wright could reasonably argue that as a senior official of the union with long experience as a full-time officer and a previous candidate for the general secretaryship he was still eligible, aged fifty-five, to run again for the top job. So why not seize the moment at the annual political showpiece of the Labour Movement? In status terms he could justifiably claim to be best qualified to succeed Todd and, compared with Bill Morris, a senior figure in trade union and Labour Party affairs. Moreover Wright was always kept fully informed and up to date on the deep controversies within the union, from the Left and the Right, that had persistently questioned the suitability of Bill Morris to take over from Todd. From Wright's point of view, even allowing for his continued admiration for his old protégé, the Wales region chief saw the possibility of winning the election campaign as an irresistible attraction. But his misjudgement, as things turned out, did not concern the merits of his claim but rather his tactics. In the end they almost certainly backfired on Wright.

Todd played his cards quite differently. He refused to be hassled. He delayed his moment to announce the election for succession for several months after Wright launched his personal broadside. Todd's timing on 7 February came five months after George Wright's Labour Party conference drama; and in that interval Todd worked quietly but shrewdly to help strengthen the claims of his chosen man, Bill Morris.

It remains arguable whether Wright would have been wiser to have waited. No one will ever know. He was without question a very strong candidate for the top job. His reputation as one of the union's most qualified negotiators was well based. He knew he could count on strong support across the political spectrum both within the union and from important figures in the Labour Party who were not natural allies of either Todd or Morris. Nor did Wright feel any impediment because of his earlier friendship with Bill Morris. In the struggle for power to lead the most important trade union in the country, with historic, political as well as industrial muscle, there was little room to demonstrate any old-fashioned sentiment toward a protégé. Few contests for the top role in a British trade union at that time carried anything like the same degree of personal, political and indeed social significance as that battle between Bill Morris and George Wright in 1991.

Now consider the broader political scene while this crucial trade union election campaign was taking place. It was at the climax of Margaret Thatcher's reign as Britain's Prime Minister. John Major was about to take over leadership of the government. We now know, albeit in retrospect, that the country was on the verge of a general election in 1992 – an election that would put to the ultimate test the electorate's verdict on Mrs Thatcher's eleven years in office. The Labour Party under Neil Kinnock had high hopes of winning that election. But of course the Labour leadership was entirely aware of public sensitivity on the question of the trade union role in society and especially of the Labour Party's umbilical links with the unions. All these elements were present, even if at subconscious level, during the Bill Morris/ George Wright fight for control of the TGWU.

When George Wright opened his campaign at the end of September 1990 he described his political position as 'centre left' but also emphasised his support for Neil Kinnock and Kinnock-style policies. He refuted some claims that he was 'the candidate of the political Right' and based his election agenda on modernising the Transport Workers Union, providing it with 'a professional style of leadership' and making the 'the union more effective and financially sound'. In a radio interview in May 1991, shortly before the ballot took place, Wright denounced those elements in the campaign who had raised racialist questions about Bill Morris's suitability. In that BBC Radio Wales interview of 5 May 1991 Wright condemned what he described as 'the race card' and declared: 'I know who's played the race card. It's been played by Bill's supporters in the desperate hope of whipping up some kind of anger about it. Racism is evil; it's repugnant. I want no part of it. I don't seek to exploit it and I seek no advantage from it. I am with Bill on that.'

That was an important statement by George Wright and wholly in line with his record in the union – not least his earliest support for the young Bill Morris. Even so it would be absurd to dismiss the fact that racial issues did play a part in that critical election. The evidence of an undercurrent of opposition to Morris on little more than racial prejudice was clearly present. Everyone concerned in that election process knew it however much they regretted and/or denied it. A senior national officer of the TGWU who still prefers to remain anonymous told the author: 'I am still disgusted, after all this time, by what was without doubt outright racialist attitudes against Bill Morris in that election – and subsequently.' This is a view underlined frequently by Ray Collins, the union's assistant general secretary in charge of its national administration.

Yet throughout all this psychological pressure Morris

remained calmly controlled, at least on the surface. He repeatedly insisted that he was not 'the black candidate' but the candidate 'who happens to be black'. From the outset Bill Morris set out his stall as candidate with absolute candour. His launching declaration made on that same 7 February emphasised the central point that underpinned his credentials: 'The fact that the country's biggest trade union elected a black worker from Birmingham as its deputy general secretary shows the TGWU to be a healthy and progressive union. I believe that the maturity and responsibility of our members will be further demonstrated when they elect me as the union's next general secretary. Our members deserve a union with a leader who guarantees opportunity for each and every one of them. I am pledged to deliver that union, that vision and that leadership.' There was no ducking or hedging the fundamental issue; he was a candidate and he was black. Take me as I am. That was the Morris message. Morris placed his unique role as the first black worker to challenge for any top job in the British trade union movement firmly at the forefront of his campaign. There was a second string to this element in his election campaign – invoking the name of Frank Cousins. Several of Morris's election leaflets carried a photograph of Cousins and Morris on the front page with the headline: 'Bill Morris for general secretary, winning for our members. In the tradition of Frank Cousins.' It was a bold enterprise – though in the opinion of some of his opponents 'a slick piece of public relations'. Morris refused to be put off by such comments. One of his most compelling election leaflets contained a section on Frank Cousins and his achievements as a reforming general secretary of the TGWU. Morris drew heavily on his hero's reputation. For example: 'Without Frank Cousins I would never have begun my life as a trade union activist and without the encouragement he offered to ordinary workers in his union I would never have become a union official. The second way in which he changed my life was his engagement in the anti-racist struggle. Upon his retirement as TGWU general secretary he became chairman of the Community Relations Council, the forerunner of the Commission for Racial Equality. In the period after Enoch Powell had poisoned British politics with his "Rivers of Blood" speech Cousins's engagement in the opposite direction was symbolic and a huge encouragement to all black workers.'

This theme, we might almost call it the 'Cousins factor', continued to play a prominent role throughout Bill Morris's election campaign. It almost certainly had a positive effect in his favour though it is impossible to offer any measure of its real significance. What can be said is that it may well have been envied, and in some cases was certainly resented, by his opponents and critics. To that extent he was able to turn what may have appeared a handicap into a plausible advantage. That election leaflet referring to Cousins certainly led to media publicity and agitation from Morris's critics. In fact one national newspaper columnist used it to promote the virtues of George Wright. Several other national newspapers picked up a similar theme arguing that the union would be far better managed by Wright. Yet, despite all this, there was strong media support for Morris, reflecting considerable praise both for the union and the man in having the courage to face up to their critics and condemning the squalid undertones that were running through the campaign.

There were four candidates seeking to succeed Ron Todd when the ballot was counted on Friday, 7 June 1991: George Wright who polled 83,059; Bob Harrison the union's national secretary for the food, drink and tobacco trades, who polled 29,882; Pat Reilly, a rank and file dairy worker from Kent who polled 12,994; and Bill Morris who triumphed with a vote of 118,206.

The turnout was 22.5 per cent, a poor and unsatisfactory response from the union's membership which then registered 1,240,000 eligible voters. Even by the normal standards of trade union elections it was a disappointing turnout for what had been a highly publicised and controversial campaign; but there was no doubt about the positive response in favour of Morris. What was more surprising was the relatively low vote for George Wright. The assumption had been for a much closer margin between Bill Morris and George Wright. The large absentee vote was clearly a big factor. Some observers saw this as an indication of what might loosely be described as 'positive neutrality' on the issue of racial prejudice. But much more likely was the traditional tendency among the average trade unionist simply to shrug the shoulders and not bother to vote. That could equally be described as 'positive apathy' rather than 'positive neutrality'. Ron Todd described the result, somewhat exaggeratedly, as 'a major exercise in democracy'. It was certainly not that; far more an exercise in trying to combat trade union, and even general social, prejudice. If Todd had made the point in congratulating Morris on his victory he would have been better advised, and justified, to have praised the sheer hard work and dedicated commitment of hundreds of rank and file TWGU members, and some officials, who were determined to overcome the routine, shallow prejudices that had marred Bill Morris's long fight for equal recognition as a genuinely effective and successful union official. That indeed was the truth. There had been a remarkable effort from a large number of TGWU rank and file members to help Morris win that election. Many rank and file members, white as well as black, were determined to canvas for Morris and speak out against his critics.

Bill Morris was not by character a demonstrative person; he rarely allowed his emotions to be on public display. Yet underneath that reserve he knew that his success and historic achievement had not been reached without pain and difficulty among his supporters. His 'thank you' statement to the union's members refrained from reflecting that measure of feeling. He kept it simple and to the point by setting out his overriding priorities' when taking over from Ron Todd. These would include 'urgent action to bring the union's finances into balance; rebuilding our membership base through organising, recruiting and mergers, and assisting in the election of a Labour government'. Morris delivered that declaration on 2 July 1991. He still had to wait another eight months until March the following year before actually taking over from Todd, and while they worked closely together in the interim it wasn't feasible for Morris to put his new plans into action until he was actually sitting in the general secretary's chair. Then the big sweep of the Morris period started to take shape. But if anyone assumed – though Bill Morris was not among them – that his biggest battles were over they were in for a surprise.

One of the first to congratulate Bill Morris on his success was George Wright. His old mentor sent a personal note to Morris explaining that he thought it best for them to have 'stayed away' from each other during the campaign. But he made no qualification in congratulating his protégé and pledging to 'throw my support' behind Morris in the bid to unite the union and especially in tackling the serious financial difficulties requiring immediate attention. It was an honest and genuine approach from Wright to help mend bridges in the interests of the union. He knew, as much as Morris, that the TGWU faced serious problems financially, organisationally and in developing, and adjusting itself, to a more modern strategy. Indeed as matters evolved it was clear that Wright was even better informed than Morris about the attempts to disrupt, unsettle and even dislodge the new general secretary. These were to come not from Wright's 'centre left' supporters but from an extraordinary combination of Tony Blair 'modernisers' on the right of the Labour Party and groupings of 'broad left' (and even ultra left) critics of Morris. The campaign – and that, eventually, is what it became – began within a year of Morris taking over from Todd and was triggered by the new leader's policies to correct the financial crisis within the TGWU and, as part of that policy, to reshape the union's organisational structure across all its regions.

Morris's first move was to stop the financial rot – a situation he inherited from his predecessor. There was an immediate deficit of £12 million to correct. In fact the union's finances had reached such a parlous state that within days of Morris taking over, its bankers, the Co-operative Unity Bank, informed the new general secretary that he could no longer sign any cheques. So serious was the deficit that the bank told Morris they would refuse to honour cheques paid without their authority – despite the fact that the TGWU's national assets, liquid as well as in property, were still huge, standing at well over £30 million. The regional secretaries also retained substantial resources in their local coffers. There was never any risk of bankruptcy but nor was there any doubt about the immediate financial gravity. Morris had to act quickly and he did. He took advice and appointed a group of financial experts from outside the union to handle the problems – a decision that was to cause him endless future trouble.

Bill Morris appointed a man called Peter Regnier, a former senior figure at British Leyland when the British Motor Corporation was run by Sir Michael Edwardes. It was not a popular move. Regnier's role initially was to join the staff of the TGWU as adviser to the finance department, then run by Harry Timpson, a long-standing and admired senior figure in the union. In addition Regnier had direct access to Bill Morris, yet he faced immense problems from the start – not con-fined to the union's financial affairs. He was inevitably resented by Timpson and the finance department as well as the union's General Executive who, by defini-tion, were also suspicious of outside 'interference'. But he was supported by Ray Collins, then assistant general secretary in charge of the union's administration and the man closest to Bill Morris at the top of the TGWU. Given the tense situation at senior levels of the union, what then followed over the next two years of financial and structural re-organisation was probably inescap-able. To this day the dispute about, and the measured assessment of, Peter Regnier's work remains a hot and contentious issue. There was no overall agreement then – or even now. But there can be no doubt about the impact of Regnier's influence. Along with Bill Morris and Ray Collins the structure and shape of the TGWU was transformed. Morris claims, with considerable jus-tice on his side, that the reconstruction he designed had saved the union. His critics, hardly surprisingly, claim that in the process of saving the union financially he undermined and damaged the old structure of the

TGWU. These critics will give credit to both Morris and Regnier for recouping funds that had been owed to the union; for changing the union's property portfolio and for freeing up union assets that had lain dormant or worse for years. But on the crucial question of reducing the union's regional groups from eleven to eight and enforcing early retirement on some senior figures including regional secretaries – on that issue Bill Morris has never been forgiven by his critics. Nor were they ready to take into account that Morris's inheritance left him with virtually no viable option. Throughout the closing years of Todd's leadership the drain on funds had become evident along with declining membership. Yet the powerful, influential General Executive – on which sat many of Morris's critics – had largely ignored the growing problem or simply offered fatuous excuses to avoid painful action. Morris inherited all that indecisiveness and set about trying to correct it. It was as if the old, traditional leadership had consciously refused to acknowledge a changing world – the steady decline in all trade union membership, notably in the TGWU, following Margaret Thatcher's legislative assault – and convinced themselves that these effects were merely a temporary blip rather than something much more fundamental. This was, to be sure, very much the attitude of Ron Todd's generation of trade union leaders – and with good reason. It was an issue that led to serious divisions within the trade union movement and the Labour Party, culminating in Blair's 'New Labour' syndrome. The irony in all this remains that it was precisely the changing social scene, with its economic and political implications, that had helped Bill Morris to rise above the earlier prejudices. Morris came to office as a committed socialist and a moderate left-wing leader. But equally as someone who recognised the need to modernise, to adapt to changing social mores and to try to rebuild and recast Britain's largest trade union to handle this changing world. It would prove a difficult task. In his own words: 'When I took over our bank had lost confidence in the union's ability to finance its activities. We were only about thirty per cent viable. That was my challenge. But I was no magician, no messiah. I simply had to face the realities of my inheritance. When I was told that I could no longer sign any more cheques I knew that something drastic was needed. So I acted swiftly and of course that did upset some people.'

Indeed it did. Perhaps no more dramatic example of this, hitherto unpublicised, was the withdrawal of support for Bill Morris from the TGWU's legendary former leader Jack Jones, the man who had succeeded Frank Cousins in transforming the union from an old-style conformist and politically orthodox power in the Labour Movement to a radical left-wing innovative force. For Morris the realisation that he no longer had the approval of the grand figure of TGWU authority, indeed a Labour Movement icon, was a severe and still more a deeply saddening blow.

But, of course, Jack Jones came from a generation of trade union leaders who were groomed and shaped by their experiences in the thirties; by the Spanish Civil

War in which Jones fought against Franco's fascists as an International Brigadier and was badly wounded, and again during the post-1945 struggles when the trade unions worked with a Labour government to repair the social and economic wounds of their bitter pre-war experience. It was a different agenda and a different mood from that which faced Bill Morris and his generation. Morris had always admired Jones and his achievements. But Jones retired before Margaret Thatcher started her assault on the trade unions. Much had changed and that made it difficult for the two strands, the Jones and Morris perceptions, to come together. The truth is that Jack Jones reflected, more so than Morris, the views, feelings, history and traditions of the TGWU executive – though not their racial prejudices. This can help explain why Jones would have preferred to see George Wright succeed Todd. That, too, was a saddening experience for Bill Morris as he began his campaign to modernise and change the union. Wright's experience from the shop floor onwards had been engraved by the old traditions of the TGWU. In that sense Bill Morris was much more the 'moderniser' whose life experience and background had moulded a quite different persona. In fact Morris possessed these qualities to such a degree that one might assume he would have offered an instinctive appeal to the new Labour leader Tony Blair; but that is not what happened.

7

The Battle at the Top

WITHIN DAYS OF BILL MORRIS taking command of the
Transport and General Workers Union the then Prime
Minister, John Major, announced a general election for
2 April 1992. It was Major's follow-through from the
drama of Margaret Thatcher's departure after thirteen
years in a reign that had transformed the British political scene. Morris registered the point and got on with
his supreme challenge of reforming and modernising what was still Britain's largest trade union despite
the havoc of the Thatcher years. He also realised that
chance had offered him a psychologically opportune
moment. By focusing on the union's immediate attention in seeking to help Neil Kinnock to win the election for the Labour Party, he could also begin work
developing a new strategy for the future of the TGWU.
Circumstances had given this apparent push-start to
Morris's battle to change the union. At least that was
a reasonable assumption. Events turned out to be far
more problematic and threatening.

There were two major elements to Morris's plan in reshaping the union and they were inextricably bound together. The urgent first task, as mentioned earlier, was to correct the financial drain and remedy the £12 million deficit on the current account. The second was to modernise the structure of the union by cleaning up some of the deadwood, much of which had simply grown up like topsy over generations since Ernest Bevin's time. The first could not be achieved without the second. Morris set about the task immediately while also conducting the union's campaign to help Neil Kinnock's election fight. But, alas, the result of the 1992 general election was a massive disappointment to Kinnock and the Labour Party leadership – and, by definition, a blow to Bill Morris's plans and hopes. He, in common with most trade union leaders had envisaged a Labour victory followed by a period of repair to damage inflicted on the trade unions during the Thatcher years. It didn't happen. John Major secured an overall majority of twenty-one in a vote which registered a 77.67 per cent turnout, an unusually high electoral response. The Conservative vote held up surprisingly well by producing 336 seats to Labour's 271, with a small gain for the Liberal Democrats who secured twenty seats in the new Parliament. It was the fourth successive Tory victory and by any measure a serious setback for the hopefuls in the trade unions. Another five years of Conservative government was ahead of them, during which they would face a continuation of Thatcherite policies. Kinnock quit the role of Labour leader and the

Party elected John Smith who after a mere two years as Labour leader died suddenly, ushering in a completely fresh political agenda called 'New Labour' under the leadership of the young Tony Blair. By 1994 when Blair was elected Labour leader the entire political scene had been transformed from the hopes and aspirations held by Bill Morris in that spring of 1992 when he began his bid to change the image of the TGWU.

After Kinnock's defeat in the 1992 general election Morris realised that he could expect no help from a John Major government. The anti-union legislation of the Thatcher years not only continued to dominate and limit trade union affairs, but far from easing restrictions, the Major government continued to tighten the legal grip on all union activities. Against that background Morris's task inevitably was made more difficult – but he refused to be deflected. The process of trying to identify a suitable candidate for effective financial advice was by no means straightforward. Morris sought advice from a number of sources including John Monks at the TUC. A name finally emerged as a result of a recommendation from the American trade unions: Adam Kline, a South African-born accountant who had worked for several of the American unions, notably as a consultant to the textile workers. Morris met Kline and initially was impressed. He asked Kline to draw up a fresh financial strategy and also suggest someone who could be appointed to administer the new plan. The result was far from a smooth transition. Kline's advice seemed sound enough. It was he who came up with the proposal to reconstruct the union's regional hierarchy. But there was no substantial follow-up from Kline and in the end both Bill Morris and Ray Collins were convinced that Kline was not a man they could depend on. He was dismissed and disappeared from the scene, though not before he had identified someone who turned out to be a considerable success: Peter Regnier, a name not then known in the union, in short an 'outsider'.

As already mentioned Regnier had held a senior post in the management of British Leyland at Longbridge. He was known to some of the union's Midlands region officials but had left no strong impression on any of them. Regnier was said to be a Labour supporter and appeared to have sound credentials as a financial operator – albeit with no previous experience of trade union internal affairs. Hitherto the TGWU finance department had been run mainly by union officials rather than qualified accountants. The man in charge of the finance department, Harry Timpson, was a popular long-serving official who had run his department competently and could not be held responsible for the build-up of a large deficit due largely to falling union membership as well as rising costs. It was also Timpson's responsibility to report on all financial affairs to the General Executive Council whose influence remained a powerful factor in all the union's operations. This meant that everyone at executive level of the union's affairs was well aware of the financial problems when Regnier moved in. What was missing from his critics' agenda was a determined policy to correct the situation. This is what a combination of Regnier and Ray Collins under the leadership of Bill Morris set out to provide.

By the same token Regnier, 'the outsider' (a derogatory label which stuck with him), became the 'blame figure' among those who opposed Morris's plans to restructure the union. The dislike, or more precisely the distrust, of Regnier by virtually all the hierarchy (apart from Bill Morris and Ray Collins) overshadowed his achievements. His early successes in reducing the union's liabilities and raising more revenue were brushed aside. One difficulty was that Regnier's precise role was never clearly defined. He did not have the authority to usurp Timpson nor did he carry an executive responsibility as defined by the rule book. He was 'Bill Morris's man about the place'. That inevitably led to Regnier being regarded with increased suspicion. He was bracketed with Morris as being responsible for cutting back on the union's eleven regions and reducing the influence of the powerful regional secretaries. Bill Morris refused to be deflected by local sentiment as he proceeded with cutting back the cost of supporting eleven regional headquarters, each with its own elaborate system of local responsibility and command of its own budget. The biggest hurdle Morris had to overcome was to persuade the union's executive to reduce these regional power centres down to eight. But for Morris this was an essential strategy in his prime objective to modernise the TGWU and reshape its finances. It meant, of course, that many of the personnel were given early retirement or offered other jobs in the union.

Union offices were closed and sold off in a widespread wave of lucrative property deals. Some of the deposed regional secretaries who were pensioned off early not only deeply resented Morris's revolution but continued to plot and fight against their general secretary. At the same time it was difficult for the union's national leadership to ignore the marked improvement in financial affairs emerging from the changes. Yet far from making the trio of Morris, Collins and Regnier more popular, it had the reverse effect. It consolidated the opposition by bringing broad left critics into an alliance with centre right influences whose common purpose became focused on one objective; to remove Bill Morris from general secretaryship of the TGWU. Collins was also under fire since he was regarded as a key figure, alongside Morris, in helping to secure Regnier's appointment. As an assistant general secretary who had literally grown up within the union machine at headquarters, Ray Collins was also seen as a vital support element for Morris. He had previously been close to Ron Todd and was known to have played a key role in assisting Todd to help advance the role of Bill Morris. All these factors were gathering together through 1993 and into 1994 as Morris, with few allies, struggled to reshape the TGWU. Inevitably the union's membership was slipping as the industrial pattern of Britain changed, with older manufacturing industries in sharp decline. Trade union organisation in the newer, technologically-based industrial developments was far lower than in old traditional industries. All unions suffered – in many ways the once mighty TGWU was weakened more than most. During Margaret Thatcher's years in power the TGWU membership had slumped by about 750,000; and the drain did not subside when she left Downing Street. By the mid-nineties the union was down to about one million members, half of what it had been in the days of the legendary Jack Jones. In fact, the resentment of Morris among the older hierarchy on the General Executive tended to increase regardless of the union's significantly improved financial condition. A solid group among the thirty-nine executive members remained scornful of Morris's restructuring of the regional groupings, regarding his strategy as unnecessary and placing too much power in a new central command of the union which they believed was also weakening the General Executive's powers. As far as Morris's critics were concerned few if any of the changes were justified. Yet Morris has never retreated from the belief that it was precisely these changes that ultimately helped save the TGWU from a far more serious crisis. Nor has he ever diluted his praise for Peter Regnier's contribution. Morris says of Regnier: 'He was a top class operator with long experience. I tell you, I regarded the appointment of Regnier and his team as one of the most important, if not *the* most important, in my time as general secretary of the TGWU. Regnier and his team helped to turn round the financial state of the union and the result was that we ended up stronger financially than any other trade union in the country.' That is conclusive praise indeed. Yet not sufficient to satisfy Morris's critics let alone what had by then become an endemic opposition to Regnier.

One of Morris's main strengths in fighting the criticism levelled against him was that neither the broad left or even the right had any serious or credible alternative solutions – except for the repeated generalisation that Morris's strategy should be based on recruiting new members and restoring the union's membership to its old heights. The complaint that Morris's strategy had failed to put a recruitment drive at the top of its agenda remained a focal point among his critics. Indeed it became the main issue and a key weapon in the armoury of Morris's opponents – ignoring the problems inflicted by the Thatcher and Major legislation which had not only severely restricted trade union activities across all British industry making union recruitment far more difficult than previously, but also, and with telling impact, concentrated on encouraging foreign investment into Britain with the attractions of lower costs, lower wages and weakened trade union resistance. It was this combination of external political handicap, allied to the resentment of the 'old guard' establishment within the traditional structure of the TGWU, that created so much anguish for Bill Morris in his first term as Todd's successor. It needs to be recognised that throughout the 1980s Margaret Thatcher's government introduced eight successive Acts of Parliament, all assigned to limit, reduce and in some cases eliminate the power and influence of all British trade unions.

If one looks for a single factor, a talisman point, at which the anti-Morris campaign gained broader strength it was in the decision to sell off the TGWU's historic home of Transport House, the building in Smith Square within a few minutes' walk of Parliament. Transport House had been opened in May 1928 by Ernest Bevin and the then Labour leader Ramsay MacDonald. It was once the heart of the Labour Movement because the TGWU from an early stage had rented out space inside the building, both to the Labour Party and the TUC, as well as the Co-operative Movement. In that context Transport House became, literally, a national cornerstone of the Labour Movement. In the case of the Labour Party and TUC both, during the 1930s, established their national headquarters at Transport House where, effectively, they were tenants of the TGWU. Of course this also added to the prestige of 'Bevin's Union'. Even if half-jokingly it allowed Bevin and his lieutenants to describe themselves as the landlords of the Labour Movement. It was a quip often thrown out by Bevin to tease or even at times intimidate his tenants. The fact that the tenants eventually departed in the post-war years to set up their own independent headquarters elsewhere in London, well before Bill Morris's tenure, did not soften the criticism about its sale. Many TGWU officials at all levels saw the sale of Transport House as sacrilege: or to use Harold Macmillan's famed description when he attacked Margaret Thatcher's privatisation policies, it was seen as 'selling off the family silver'. Bill Morris remained unrepentant. He saw the sale as an inescapable part of repairing the finances of the union and reshaping the TGWU. He perhaps also regarded the sale, if only subconsciously, as a clear psychological marker that times were changing, and selling Transport House became a form of token in his determination to change the union and its image. To this day he defends the sale of the historic nine-storey building as an 'absolute essential requirement' in his bid to rescue the union's finances. Morris insists: 'The place was badly run-down and in need of much repair and modernisation. We estimated the cost of doing this work would be £16 million, and that was in 1994. The place needed considerable structural rebuilding. There were no car-parking facilities and all the social amenities were far below recognised standards including even the toilets. It was a nightmare. The sensible solution was to sell it at a good price and move to a more modern building with up-to-date facilities. That is why we moved – despite the sentiment.' According to Bill Morris Transport House raised £10 millions from which the union then bought, refashioned and modernised its current Theobalds Road headquarters for £6 million. 'It was,' Morris argues, 'a very good deal indeed.' The new headquarters was also given the old brand name of Transport House.

Set against this argument were the traditionalists – men like former national officer Brian Revell whose political and industrial instincts were strongly on the Left and someone who can firmly be regarded as well removed from racial prejudice. Yet Revell voted for

George Wright in the election for Todd's successor and regarded such things as the sale of Transport House as a cardinal error of judgement by Morris. He says: 'The selling of Transport House was the worst thing that happened to the TGWU in my opinion. Bill Morris was never forgiven for that.' In fact Morris insists that the sale of Transport House was a crucial element in returning the union's finances to a healthy condition.

The new headquarters was a purpose-built modern building not far from the TUC headquarters. While it was being built the union took temporary accommodation in a modern high-rise building in Palace Street close to Victoria in January 1995. Few national officials approved of the temporary move, or even the new headquarters project. Yet in truth by then there was little Morris could have done to win approval from his critics, who gladly seized on every opportunity, however minor, to complain about the strategy, tactics and personal conduct of their general secretary. In an interview Ray Collins made this brutally candid observation: 'Quite frankly the plotting had become endemic; and so was the racialism. I was disgusted and I still am by the anti-Bill Morris racialism on all sides and sadly across the political spectrum.'

Throughout all the criticism and the clamour Morris remained steadfast. No one was closer to Bill Morris than Ray Collins throughout the whole of this internal turmoil; no one was better able to judge the man in the eye of the storm: Collins verdict is that Bill 'had great courage'.

Towards the end of 1994 as the union departed its old shrine of Transport House it was already apparent that something drastic was required to quell the storm of criticism and internal plotting against Bill Morris by a continuing critical faction. But the trigger for the dramatic events that swept across the union in the next twelve months was the sudden death, in May 1994, of the Labour leader John Smith. In the two years following Neil Kinnock's defeat at the 1992 election Smith had developed a strong new relationship with trade union leaders, not least with Bill Morris. His death brought about a fundamental shift in that relationship. When Tony Blair was elected to lead the Labour Party he embarked on a completely new agenda. The focal point of the Blair revolution was to change the whole direction of the Labour Movement towards a policy of reform in the nature and character of the Labour Party. Much of the emphasis would be put on distancing the new Blair leadership from the traditions of 'old-style Labour' – especially the historic links with the trade unions. One of Blair's first moves was to announce at the 1994 Labour Party autumn annual conference – his inaugural as leader – a proposal to amend the Party's Clause 4, which set out its founding principles. In brief, Clause 4 was akin to a form of biblical declaration. It was regarded mainly as stating the guiding socialist ethos underpinning the Labour Party – that of bringing major areas of the economy under public ownership. From Labour's origins this had been the creed, an essential tablet of faith, even if in practice it always remained, largely, a theoretical objective. Most of Labour's leaders had in the past viewed Clause 4 as a kind of silent reminder of an old idealistic dream – yet hardly realistic in modern times. But for Labour's radical and left wing the existence of Clause 4 was a constant insurance policy against political treachery by the moderates and reformers. Blair set out to change all that by abolishing the Clause. His argument was that its very existence alienated 'Middle England' where he believed the Party's future support should be based. He also believed that presenting the voters with its abolition would become a major advantage factor in the next general election by persuading the floating voters that 'New Labour' was no longer the ideological force it once was. It was certainly the most radical proposal ever put forward since the Party's constitution was drawn up during the First World War. It heralded the beginning of Blair's revolution. The trade unions, in the main, were opposed to such a change and made their opposition quite clear. They believed it was an unnecessary abandonment of the Party's faith. Blair called a special conference to fight the issue in open debate. That was held in London during Easter 1995 and he won the majority he needed to confirm the abolition of Clause 4, replacing it with a series of generalised platitudes. There was much confusion and internal strife within all the unions before – and after – that vote. For weeks before the special conference the unions had carried out internal tests of their members' views. Bill Morris organised what he described as 'a sounding out' of members across the union's 6,000 branches. He did not conduct a full membership ballot as the Blairite supporters were demanding. Instead Morris claimed that testing the views across all the TGWU branches had been sufficient to produce a clear rejection of Blair's proposed changes. Of course his claim was dismissed by his critics as dubious or at best inadequate – chiefly by Blair supporters as well as in the right-wing press.

At the special conference held in Central Hall Westminster, Morris used the TGWU's powerful block vote against Blair's plans – but narrowly lost the final vote. To this day that Central Hall vote remains a disputed verdict. Some observers – including Rodney Bickerstaffe, the former leader of UNISON, the public service union – are still convinced that Blair's plan was defeated but was mistakenly counted, accidentally or otherwise. Bickerstaffe had already allied himself with Bill Morris in opposition to Blair and he stands convinced they had beaten Blair in that crucial vote. He says: 'I have no doubt that we defeated Blair on that vote.' Morris agrees that all the prior indications had pointed to a Blair defeat. Yet the reality is that, since then, history has been written and built on the basis of a Blair triumph – a triumph which became the principal foundation stone in Tony Blair's reformation of New Labour. Bickerstaffe and Morris may retain, as they do, their disbelief, but the scene has moved on. What is undeniable is that this event confirmed what was probably inevitable – a mutual political distrust between Blair and Morris, and indeed between Blair and those unions and union leaders who opposed his changes. It was a distrust that was to lead to Blair and his advisers moving into an extraordinary alliance with those inside the TGWU hierarchy who were plotting against Morris. An alliance which, once more, presented Bill Morris with another, perhaps far larger, challenge to his role as leader of the TGWU. This time it not only involved racial prejudice but added to it a deep rift in attitudes towards the political future of the Labour Party and its relations with the trade unions. For Morris it was a new and massive test of his courage and resourceful leadership. And it produced a combination of both.

The various alliances building up against Morris in 1994 consisted largely of coalitions of political and tribal convenience, some of them almost laughably improbable, others quite absurd. But they had the effect of forcing Morris and his advisers to produce a highly unusual and quite remarkable counter-offensive. The Morris camp played a trump card by bringing forward by one year the timing of the scheduled re-election for TGWU general secretaryship. The irony was that they were able to do this thanks to Margaret Thatcher's legislation requiring regular five-yearly elections by secret membership ballots. Morris would not, in fact, have been required to put his leadership to the test until 1996, but he was able to use a loophole in the new laws that enabled the union to be flexible in choosing the timing of such a ballot. It was a device that he and his supporters used with dramatic effect to scupper the attempts to displace him.

All routine assumptions had been based on Morris's re-election campaign being launched towards the end of 1995 – in fact shortly after the union's Biennial Delegate Conference in July that year. Of course this would have accomodated those who were planning to use the BDC as a major launching pad for disrupting the Morris leadership. To counter all this plotting the 'one-year-earlier' tactic was a brilliant move by a small group of those around Bill Morris, notably Ray Collins and his allies, to outmanoeuvre the plotters on all sides of the extraordinary alliance of opposites – both outside as well as inside the TGWU. The broad left campaign against Morris within the union was led by a talented and impressive, rank and file, communist member of the General Executive, Peter Hagger. He had powerful support from full-time national officials including the deputy general secretary Jack Adams – who had filled that vacancy when Morris was elected general secretary; Bobby Owens, the regional secretary in the north-west and a member of the Liverpool-based far left Militant Tendency, and John Freeman the regional secretary in Ireland.* This led an extremely powerful group with a single objective – to remove Bill Morris

* The TGWU history is of a mixed and often confused relationship with the Republic of Ireland. For a long time after its formation in 1922 the union had membership in the Republic where it was known as the Amalgamated TGWU. There had been a quite separate TGWU from 1913, but not associated with Bevin's TGWU. Some members in the Republic remained in the main union until recently. Now it is confined mainly to Northern Ireland.

from leadership of the union by denouncing his policies and forcing a vote of confidence at the BDC. The group recruited several leading figures from the centre and right of the union's executive with a plan to mount a direct challenge to Morris at the July conference in Blackpool. The Morris/Collins tactic thwarted this by calling a surprise early re-election for Morris – *before* the BDC. It was planned with the cunning and secrecy of a strategic military counter-offensive. Their plan was kept top secret until everything had been prepared. Collins then shattered the plotters by phoning several of them to announce an early date for the re-election. He began with John Freeman in Ireland who, when hearing the news, was, in Collins's words, 'left speechless'. Collins informed all regional secretaries that the election would commence on 19 May 1995 and the ballot to close on 16 June. The result was scheduled for 23 June – one week before the start of the BDC. The plotters were thrown into disarray. The time schedule left little opportunity for them to mount any significant counter-offensive – though they tried hard. The stunning move seemed to have done the trick for Bill Morris as everyone awaited the outcome of the national membership vote. Even so the anti-Morris cavalcade, despite being thrown into confusion, did not abandon their audacity. Knowing that Morris was unpopular with the Labour leader Tony Blair, the disruptive coalition sought the help of Tony Blair and his top adviser, including Lord (then Mr) Peter Mandelson, in a publicity campaign to boost a candidate in opposing Morris.

The anti-Morris group went as far as trying to persuade George Wright to stand again to remove Bill Morris, believing this would be entirely acceptable to Blair. But it backfired. When approached by the broad left leader, Peter Hagger, George Wright flatly refused to play any part in the plot. In the end the surprise candidate to contest Bill Morris in this extraordinary battle was Jack Dromey who hitherto had promised support to Morris. Dromey had several times contemplated running for high office and had in the past sought alliance with Morris. But in the end he joined those who had become disenchanted with Morris's leadership. He was in his own right a prominent and successful national officer in charge of the union's public service section – then the largest trade group in the TGWU. There was another important factor helping to persuade Dromey to pick up the challenge to Morris: he knew he could count on the backing of the Blair establishment in which his wife, Harriet Harman MP*, was a prominent figure in the shadow cabinet team. It was a formidable array of strength and conspiracy against Bill Morris; a remarkable combination of mixed motives, political disapproval, tactical disagreements and personal rivalries.

It would be understandable for any observer to assume that the threatening storm that descended over Bill Morris's leadership would have diverted him from effectively running the TGWU and continuing his programme of

---

* Now deputy leader of the Labour Party.

reform and restructuring. In fact this did not happen. There was little outward sign that his demeanour had been hijacked by the disruptive forces swirling around him. Little of the internal conflict within the TGWU had found its way into the press until the Blair/Mandelson media offensive in support of Dromey. On the surface it appeared to be a period of intense activity for Morris in his bid to change the face of the TGWU and update its performance, bringing it more in line with modern practices. One of his major campaigns, during the leadership trauma, was to launch a completely new personal service to members by providing round-the-clock free legal advice not only to individual members but also to their families.* The project covered three million people and allowed the TGWU to set a new pattern as the first British trade union to open up what in effect was a national citizen's advice service financed by the union. Morris regarded this initiative as part of his aim to increase the democratic process within the union and also a policy he described as seeking a 'New Partnership' between the union and its members. To this he added an objective of trying to persuade and encourage some of the nation's biggest employers to play their part in his plans to broaden industrial democracy. His proposal was aimed at switching away, whenever

---

* In 1994 the TGWU became the first major trade union to provide round-the-clock free legal advice to its members and their families. About three million people were involved as Bill Morris developed the scheme. It was called Helpline.

possible, from confrontational attitudes towards offering employers the opportunity to be more co-operative in their dealings with trade unions. Morris saw this as one answer to Thatcher's anti-union laws. At the same time he launched a more vigorous campaign against the national malaise of low pay and joined forces with other unions – notably Rodney Bickerstaffe's UNISON – in a major fight to establish a national minimum wage for all workers. One of his hopes had been for a Kinnock-led Labour government after the 1992 election to have introduced a statutory minimum wage. In fact this was eventually introduced by the Blair government after the 1997 general election, one of the few key concessions made to the trade unions during the Blair years.

None of this led to a diminishing of activities by his internal or external critics. His internal foes attacked Morris's proposals to employers and denounced any 'New Partnership' concept as a 'sell-out'. At the same time there were numerous industrial disputes he had to contend with, most serious and disruptive of all being a major clash in the Liverpool docks. This was a complex issue involving a small stevedore company and concerning redundancies – an issue that would have been avoidable under the old National Dock Labour Scheme which the Thatcher government had closed down. The Liverpool dock dispute was a prolonged dispute that seriously split an already troubled union. It continued into 1998 when it was abandoned amid intense bitterness. In essence it was a dispute caused entirely by the legislation drawn up during the Thatcher years which had made it doubly difficult for disputes to be resolved by negotiation and compromise. In fact the Liverpool dispute remained unresolved until 2007, some time after Morris had retired. It was one of a series of bitter feuds within the Liverpool branches of the union in a region that had continuously brought problems to Bill Morris from the moment he became general secretary. At one stage in his earlier dealings with his Liverpool members he had been compelled to expel a group of particularly militant far left activists across the Merseyside zone following evidence of financial corruption. In fact the whole Merseyside region had become a perpetual and challenging problem for Morris and was always at the top of his 'action pad'.

Yet he allowed nothing to deter him from the central task in moving ahead with restructuring the TGWU alongside playing an increasingly prominent role on the General Council of the TUC. A particularly important function in the mid-nineties was his chairmanship of a TUC special working party dealing with the extension of workers' rights on the shop floor. Bill Morris was elected chair of this TUC group called Your Voice at Work. Its secretary was David Lea (now Lord Lea of Crondall) who had been one of John Monks's senior deputies at the TUC. It was a highly prestigious group covering a wide range of trade union proposals to extend employment rights as a counter-effect to the Thatcher anti-union laws. Almost all of these additional responsibilities were coming to Morris as he fought the campaign for re-election as general secretary, the first

T&G leader to have to seek a second term in office under the terms of Margaret Thatcher's legislative agenda, and a campaign dramatised by the personal interventionist role played by the Labour leader Tony Blair.

Some of the details involved in Tony Blair's support for the candidacy of Jack Dromey are worth considering in more detail since it was an attempt without parallel to influence the removal from office of the general secretary of one of the most powerful unions in the country. From the outset Tony Blair was active behind the scenes canvassing the qualities of Dromey. In particular Blair is known to have made personal private approaches to several regional secretaries of the TGWU with whom, as a T&G member himself, he had established close connections. That in itself was, to say the least, unusual – not because it was unheard of for a Labour leader to whisper his preferences for a preferred candidate in a trade union election, or to use his influence in favouring a chosen candidate, but because in this case it involved unseating an elected general secretary. Private telephone discussions between a Labour Party leader and TGWU regional chiefs encouraging such a move were something quite exceptional. Nor was this activity confined to the Labour Party leader. Blair enlisted one of his closest political and personal advisers, Peter Mandelson, to use his long-established media connections (he had been head of media affairs for the Labour Party) to filter the same message in support of Jack Dromey. There is irrefutable evidence of Mandelson contacting a number of editors of national daily newspapers setting out the case in favour of Dromey to replace Bill Morris. To quote from Andrew Murray's recent authorised and excellent history of the union *The T&G Story*: 'The contest rapidly became confrontational; there was bitterness about an attempt to use Tory laws to unseat Britain's first black trade union leader and this was compounded by a sense that the Labour leadership was interfering in the affairs of the T&G. The actual strengths and weaknesses of Morris's record in office were overlooked in what became a totemic battle over the union's future.'

One of the national newspapers contacted by Mandelson was the *Daily Mirror* which was a traditional loyal supporter of the Labour Party and at that time still holding a huge circulation of nearly three million. On 31 May 1995 the following editorial appeared in the paper: 'Trade unions have suffered a terrible battering over the past sixteen years. They have lost five million members – almost forty per cent of their number – and seen many of their rights abolished. Few unions have suffered more than the giant T&G. But it is still of crucial importance to its members and the Labour Movement. So is the election for its general secretary.' It then goes on: 'The spirit in which the T&G election has been conducted is no great advert for modern trade unionism. It has been personalised and nasty in stark contrast with the election for the Labour leadership a year ago. But that should not dissuade members from voting. On the contrary it makes it more important for there to be a high turnout. *The Mirror* was deeply critical of the

T&G leaders' failure to ballot their members over the proposed changes to Labour's Clause 4. Now they have the chance to vote not just on that decision but on how they want their union run in future. [...] Bill Morris stands on his record. Jack Dromey sets out the changes he would make. The decision is for the members. Not only must the union's policies be right for the present climate but so must its relationship with the Labour Party. It is crucial for Tony Blair that the unions do not run the party. But neither should Labour think it can run the unions.'

It was an extremely skilful editorial; far less forcefully pro-Dromey and Blair than comments in other newspapers. Yet nonetheless cleverly tilting the paper's advice in favour of the Blair/Dromey argument for a different kind of TGWU leadership, as the paper's influential political editor Joe Haines had done in a previous article. It was a common pattern of media opinion that the Bill Morris period of leadership had failed not least in rejecting the Blair programme for a 'New Labour Party'.

In the event the triumph for Bill Morris in his re-election vote of June 1995 was a special moment in the history of British trade unions and indeed underlining the decency and common sense of rank and file democracy. The election result produced a remarkably high turnout of thirty-three per cent and the vote for Bill Morris was 158,909 compared with Jack Dromey's 100,056. A third candidate, Norman Davidson, a rank and file farmworker from Kent, polled 16,833.

Morris's comment on the result was: 'It has been difficult for the union but the membership was offered a clear choice and has made that choice by an absolutely decisive majority. I now call upon the whole T&G to unite around the agenda on which I have been elected.'

The re-confirmed general secretary clearly knew that his appeal for unity behind his programme would almost certainly fall on closed minds. Yet he had triumphed over the most contentious, bitter, distasteful trade union election for generations. Even his most inflexible critics were forced into a reluctant nod of admiration in his direction. As Ray Collins consistently claimed: 'The man had exceptional bottle'.

8

A Fight to the End

WHEN HE WAS RE-ELECTED in 1995 Bill Morris still had eight years to travel as general secretary of the T&G before his scheduled retirement date in October 2003 when he would reach the age of sixty-five. What then, at that moment, was his frame of mind? He could have been forgiven had he relapsed into a mood of deep resentment, even bitterness, after surviving such an extraordinary battle against an astonishing coalition of prejudices. He rejected that path; it would not have been in character for him to do otherwise despite all the provocation. His quality of quiet, resolute, defiant determination to prove his critics not only wrong but morally misguided overrode instincts for revenge. He immediately threw himself into work and moved into higher gear to complete his plans for the transformation of the union. Of course he was reinforced in the knowledge that he had been given an overwhelming vote of confidence by the membership. He recognised that the plotting, the sniping, the criticism, would not stop as a result of his election triumph. Yet he was also aware that he had beaten the combined opposition of Tony Blair, the far left within the union's hierarchy and his traditional right-wing opponents especially among various regional chieftains as well as a range of disgruntled national secretaries. He knew clearly where his allies were and the support he could expect from them, notably from his chief lieutenant Ray Collins, who possessed matchless skill in administration. An additional supportive factor was the retirement in 1998 of Jack Adams as deputy general secretary and his replacement by Margaret Prosser who was a strong ally of Ray Collins. Adams, who was an active member of the Communist Party, and Morris had never established anything beyond a cold formal relationship. There had been mutual distrust between them since Morris became deputy general secretary during a campaign in which Adams in his previous role as a key union official in the car industry played an important and active part in helping the plotters to destabilise Morris. The election of Margaret Prosser as his number two was a huge gain for Bill Morris. Prosser had been a most effective national women's officer and she had managed Morris's campaign to broaden the role of women members and provide them with a voice in the affairs of the T&G never before achieved. The TGWU, like most trade unions, traditionally had been a highly male-dominated union. The many years of trade union campaigning for equal pay had always been honoured more by lip service than genuine results. But times changed as more and more women moved into work and especially into industries once dominated by men. The number of women workers, in industry and in professional occupations, had now reached almost half the total of the nation's workforce. Yet to turn this statistic into a membership gain for the union was far from straightforward. Margaret Prosser had to fight gender prejudice inside the T&G to a degree almost matching Morris's battle against racial prejudice. So they had much in common and Prosser's success in recruiting women to the union led to her promotion as number two to the general secretary, bringing a powerful and refreshing reinforcement to the Morris camp. It was also further confirmation of Morris's policy in encouraging more women members by promoting women into the top ranks of the union. Prosser (now Baroness Prosser) was the first woman to reach that senior rank in the TGWU hierarchy, which established yet another 'first' for the union – standing with a black general secretary, and a woman as his number two, was a fundamental break with the past. Although the ambience around Bill Morris was now less stressed with continual tribal battles, it would remain a fight to the end.

Turn now for a moment away from Bill Morris's reinforced position in the T&G itself to consider his wider role across the political and industrial spectrum – a status heavily strengthened by his re-election. Whatever the tensions with Tony Blair, the Labour leadership and advisers around Blair recognised they now had to come to terms with Morris, like it or not. To be sure Blair kept his distance from the T&G though that was little different from his relationship with most trade unions. The Labour leader never failed to register his disdain for the unions, their culture as well as their practices. He was never 'one of them'. Even so the Labour Party needed the trade unions for its financial support, despite Blair's agenda to move closer to big business and wealthy private donations, a policy calculated to help distance his reliance on trade union support. Even so he had to recognise that the T&G was still the largest single financial prop among the unions. It was a recognition of this that brought Bill Morris the chairmanship of the important Trade Union Committee for Labour, a liaison group of Party and trade union leaders which masterminded trade union financial and practical support for all affiliated unions in helping Labour's election strategy across the country. This, along with his role as chairman of the Party Conference Arrangements Committee, put Morris into a position of substantial political influence. It even led to some surprise socialising with Tony and Cherie Blair after Blair became Prime Minister following the 1997 general election. But in the run-up to that election there remained a still considerable degree of tension as Blair kept his distance from the unions, determined as he was to persuade the voters that his 'New Labour Party' was not beholden to the trade unions as in the past.

Meanwhile Morris's position on the TUC General

Council of which he had been a member for nearly nine years when he was re-elected T&G leader in 1995 was also significantly strengthened. Two years before Morris was re-elected in 1995 John Monks had taken over as general secretary of the TUC succeeding Norman Willis. As a measure of Bill Morris's increasing stature within the TUC leadership, the story of his personal intervention in the appointment of Monks in 1993 carries important testimony. As Willis's retirement drew near a number of the old guard members of the General Council were looking round for a strong replacement. Willis's period as TUC general secretary had been badly undermined under the Thatcher years and finally by the year-long miners' strike in the mid-eighties. In those years of militant Thatcherism the TUC was left marooned, isolated and largely helpless. It was a painful situation that Norman Willis had to shoulder with fortitude and courage, often with a touch of his characteristic whimsical self-deprecating humour; but it didn't conceal his dejection. Inevitably this situation affected his status as TUC leader and as his retirement approached a group of senior General Council members did not believe the internal TUC bureaucracy was adequate to the task of finding a suitable successor as leader of the national trade union centre. This group of 'elder statesmen' sought a national trade union figure from outside the TUC's internal machine to take over from Willis and to sideline his deputy and obvious successor, John Monks. The man singled out by this group was Leif Anthony Mills, the fifty-seven-year-old general secretary of the Banking, Insurance and Finance Union, an Oxford graduate of Balliol College with strong connections in the upper reaches of the financial establishment. The TUC 'elders' saw Mills as someone better placed than the younger John Monks to restore prestige to a diminished TUC. It was a bold unorthodox and certainly reckless attempt to flout convention. The 'elders' believed they had everything sewn up when finally they approached Bill Morris, who was leader of the T&G, then still the single most powerful union within the TUC. Morris exploded with indignation at his TUC colleagues. He crushed their arguments and their plans by applauding the qualities and the leadership potential of the younger Monks, then forty-eight, and flatly refused to have anything to do with their plot to submerge Monks. Perhaps, for Morris, this attempt to sidetrack Monks reminded him of what he had faced from the plotters inside the T&G. Morris insisted not only on the legitimacy of Monks succeeding Willis but argued with great force that in any event Monks was also by far the best man for the job. The plot and plotters were demolished and John Monks became TUC general secretary – arguably becoming one of its best post-war TUC leaders after George Woodcock. It is something Monks has never ceased to recognise. He remains an admirer of Morris's courage, honesty and integrity.

Monks worked with Morris on TUC affairs almost to the time of Bill Morris's retirement in 2003. Throughout his decade at the head of the TUC he maintained a close relationship with Morris; not always a smooth or an easy friendship because of frequent inter-union conflicts. Even so the Monks/Morris relationship was always based on a mutual trust and respect. Monks often found that a large amount of his time and energy as TUC general secretary was spent in trying to resolve inter-union rivalries, especially between the T&G and other unions, notably the engineering unions (now combined in a merged body named AMICUS and part of a subsequent merger with the T&G called UNITE.

In all his dealings with the T&G leader Monks found Morris one of the most honourable of all union leaders, saying: 'I liked Bill; we were never close personal friends because Bill was a man who kept his distance, but he was someone I could trust. He was a very good TUC man, very supportive and I do not forget what he did to help me.' Monks also points out: 'It was a great tribute to the TGWU that they were the first to elect a black person as the union's general secretary.'

Brendan Barber, the current general secretary of the TUC who succeeded Monks in 2003, didn't work for long with Bill Morris before his retirement in October that year but, as Monks's deputy, he too had a long working relationship with Morris and agrees with Monks. Barber also confirms the views of other TUC figures, like Rodney Bickerstaffe, who found that Bill Morris preferred to keep his distance from any of the political and tribal factions within the TUC General Council, regardless of their left or right political tendencies. 'Bill was an excellent member of the TUC General Council and supportive of the TUC as an institution especially when we came under attack often from inside the trade union movement. Frankly he was far more supportive than some of his predecessors as TGWU general secretaries; yes, it's true he was something of a "loner" but he was also a first-class chairman of a number of our committees, notably the employment policy group which at that time was one of major committees within the TUC.'

Bill Morris's involvement with the special TUC committee on working life in Britain (Your Voice at Work), which played a prominent part in shaping future trade union policy on employment as well as laying the foundations on which the future Blair government could build, has already been mentioned. The aim of that TUC committee was to draw up a policy outline for a Labour government to introduce legislation protecting the rights of working people, including the right to belong to a trade union. The TUC motive was to try to offset much of the damage that had been inflicted on trade unions during the Thatcher years and to correlate these improvements with European legislation on workers' rights, as well as responsibilities. The Blair years did indeed see the introduction of a number of these measures – but nothing on the scale the TUC or its committee under Bill Morris had advocated.

The Labour election victory of 1997 under Tony Blair's leadership created an entirely new epoch in British political life. The magnitude of Blair's overall majority stunned the political world and even Blair himself. No previous Labour government had been elected with such an overall dominant command of the House of Commons; not even Attlee's 1945 overall majority was quite as high as Blair's 1997 victory margin. It was by any standards a remarkable performance after eighteen years of unbroken Conservative Party government, of which more than eleven had been under Margaret Thatcher's rule. Euphoria swept across the Labour Movement not least among the trade unions who had played a notable role in the campaign leading to Blair's victory. And among those unions the TGWU had, as was its tradition, played a predominant part not only in helping to finance the Labour campaign but in practical assistance in almost every constituency across Britain. Bill Morris was certainly among the cheerleaders despite his previous and highly damaging experiences with Tony Blair. He refused to allow those earlier personal issues to influence his enthusiastic welcome to the new Labour government. For the trade unions it promised a new era of hope after the dark years of Thatcherism during which trade union membership had been halved and their industrial power and influence largely destroyed. They may have had their sceptical thoughts about what a Tony Blair government might, in practice, offer them; but in those early days the union leaders kept their scepticism well concealed. Their hopes were higher than their expectations.

When the new Labour cabinet was announced the choice of Gordon Brown as Chancellor of the

Exchequer was a welcome sign for Bill Morris. Like the Labour leader himself Gordon Brown was also a member of the T&G and relations between Brown and Morris had been strong from the time Morris was first elected general secretary of the union. Once inside the Treasury, Brown continued his close relationship with Morris and shortly before his sixtieth birthday the T&G leader was invited by the new Chancellor to become a member of the Court of the Bank of England under the then governor, the late Eddie George. Once again it was 'a first' for Morris: the first black director of the Bank of England. On his appointment Bill Morris offered his usual, short remark: 'Everything I do is a first.'

What was especially interesting about Gordon Brown's decision to appoint the Transport Union leader was that, unknowingly, Bill Morris had been appointed in the face of some considerable competition – though not opposition – from other trade union leaders. One notable candidate had been Rodney Bickerstaffe whose name was put forward by another member of Blair's new cabinet, David Blunkett, who at that time held the cabinet post of education secretary. It is doubtful whether Morris knew this at the time but in any event Brown was insistent that the choice be Bill Morris.

He served for more than eight years as a member of the Bank of England directorate and was twice reappointed by Gordon Brown – an unusually long spell for any member of the Court. In fact he remained a member of the Court for nearly two years after his retirement from the T&G and continued to play a role, sometimes informally, with the new governor, Mervyn King, with whom he had established a close relationship. Indeed Governor King appointed Bill Morris deputy chairman of one of the key subcommittees of the Court, and although the formal links are now severed he continues the work he started as a member of the Court in using the vast network of Bank of England social welfare contacts to help advance young black students. In fact in all Morris chaired an additional two subcommittees of the Bank, the Bank of England pension fund committee and the remuneration committee. His links with Governor Mervyn King remain strong. 'The Bank,' says Bill Morris, understandably proud of his achievement, 'is a great institution.'

Several of those who served with Morris on the Court speak of him as a 'most impressive' member of the Court who left with a very high reputation. Yet up to the time he retired from the T&G none of these achievements, nor the accolades they evoked, helped soften the mood of his critics while he remained general secretary. They continued to snipe at him and frequently criticised Morris for taking on too many 'outside' roles, quite apart from his membership of the Bank of England Court. Further, some of the brigade of critics rebuked him for accepting membership of a Royal Commission on the Reform of the House of Lords. As in the past Morris's critics filtered their views on him with barbed phrases behind cupped hands. The gossip generated was similar to tactics used when Morris was fighting to sustain his credibility as general secretary – always seeking to undermine his authority with arguments such as: 'Bill is taking on all these outside roles to boost his credibility in the union' or 'He is taking on all these extra jobs because he regards them as demonstrating his acceptance by the Establishment.' They were simply further manifestations of the shallowness of his critics and, no doubt, their envy. Morris's response was the characteristic shrug with a very brief comment: 'What do you expect from them …?'

The three big industrial issues in the closing years of his leadership of the union were all major problems demanding the closest day-to-day attention. In order of complexity they were: trouble at Liverpool docks which turned out to be the most difficult; a major dispute with British Airways; and running across both these difficult disputes was a huge crisis over the future of the old British Leyland car plant at Longbridge – this latter exploding into a fierce internal battle with the union's national secretary for the motor car industry, Tony Woodley, who eventually came to succeed Bill Morris.

In many ways the Liverpool docks dispute was the most immediately contentious, difficult and emotionally explosive issue of any Bill Morris had to handle during his final period of leadership. This was due chiefly to the historic role the dockers had played in the history of the TGWU. The port industry and the dockers had from the start been very much Ernest Bevin's special field, the basis on which he had formed the union. It was also the industry in which Bevin first won a national reputation. But by the late eighties the port industry scene had been transformed partly by new technology and port mechanisation and again by the Thatcher government's legislation abolishing the National Dock Labour Scheme that provided job security for dockworkers. Liverpool still retained some measure of job protection, though it was much weakened. A dispute arose when a small stevedore firm at the port cut back its workforce, triggering a strike that soon involved most of the Merseyside port. It rapidly developed into a bitter three-way internal contest between local dockers, their union officials and the union's national leadership who were accused of 'selling out' the dockers to anti-union employers. The dilemma facing Bill Morris and the T&G leadership was the following: to come out in full support of the dockers' case would have flouted the new laws which in turn could have led to employers, backed by the Conservative government of the time, enforcing the law at huge financial risk to the entire union. In fact the T&G leadership did make every effort to support the dismissed (or as they described themselves 'locked out') dockers, but found the law extremely limiting. This of course didn't satisfy the striking dockers who then canvassed port workers across the world and succeeded in winning considerable support. It became a political as well as an industrial *cause célèbre* and exploded violently at the 1997 Biennial Delegate Conference of the T&G. A large group of Liverpool dockers invaded the conference at Brighton to harangue and barrack the union's leadership. Some of them were admitted to the conference and sat in the gallery chanting racial slogans at Bill Morris. They were demanding supportive action not only from their union but also from the newly elected Blair government. But ministers had already made it clear that the government would not intervene to change the law. Morris was trapped in an impossible deadlock between his members, the law and the government's refusal to get involved. The Liverpool dispute was abandoned in 1998 – though that didn't end the strife or the bitterness. Some of the Liverpool dockers then pursued legal action against the T&G itself and were supported by various extreme left-wing groups, one of whose leaders had been expelled from the union for alleged financial corruption during Bill Morris's first term as general secretary. In fact the Liverpool dock strike eventually developed into an embittered contest between left-wing factions on Merseyside and Morris himself – elements of which had already been manifest in the extraordinary re-election campaign of 1995. There was also a good measure of provocative media support for the dockers' case and criticism of the way the issue had been handled by Morris and the TGWU – an ironic twist since the media traditionally were hostile to strikes and strikers, especially dockers. Even some of Bill Morris's allies and friends were also critical of the way the dispute had been handled. The Liverpool docks crisis was never effectively resolved although in 2007, four years after Morris had retired, a settlement of a kind was reached, though to this day the shadow remains.

The British Airways dispute was an entirely different matter which turned into a major industrial success for the union and personally for Bill Morris. It focused on British Airways' attempt to change the whole structure and relationship with its cabin crews. The company, one of the largest in Britain and intent on cost-cutting, sought to make large reductions in staffing by cutting the pay and reducing working conditions of flight stewards and stewardesses. In the process BA management, which itself had been restructured since privatisation, decided to get tough with the union, an attitude born from the industrial culture of the Thatcher years. Some of the top BA chiefs would have liked to get rid of unionisation altogether and they encouraged a small organisation called Cabin Crew 89 as a union-breaking tool. This group warned their recruits that they would face dismissal if they went on strike against the BA plans for cutting back. In the event the majority of cabin crew members remained in the T&G and, in 1997, went on strike for three days. Their action forced British Airways chief Bob Ayling to retreat. The company came to an agreement with the union very quickly afterwards and provided the T&G and Bill Morris with an industrial success at a time when such trade union achievements were extremely rare. It was a victory for Morris which he could deservedly savour. In one of the media interviews he gave after his British Airways success Bill Morris replied to a *Financial Times* journalist who asked whether he regarded the BA chief Bob Ayling as 'an enemy': 'Oh no, no, no. We've [Bob Ayling and Morris] never lost touch during this dispute. It wasn't bitter. It was a dispute about principles. The two qualities I bring to any relationship are my personal integrity and my respect.' The journalist challenged him again suggesting that that sounded a bit too sanctimonious and went on to question him about his religious and moral attitudes: 'I am not practising.' Morris said of his religious links. 'I don't rush off to Church every day. But I have my own values. I believe in truth, honesty. Everyday values that most people live by.'

These values were put to a severe test a little later when he was faced with the beginning of the decline of the British motor car industry and indeed what eventually proved to be the end for the famed former British Leyland and British Motor Corporation plant at Longbridge that once employed nearly 40,000 workers. In the mid-eighties the group was effectively taken over by the Thatcher government in an extraordinary ideological *volte face* to save the company from collapse, and was renamed the Rover Group. It remained the largest single British-owned car manufacturer with its main production centres at Longbridge, Birmingham and Cowley, Oxford. But despite all effort by several governments this once-famed car group, one of the industry's originals, simply couldn't turn round the economics of their car production. World competition, especially from Japan and Germany, was gradually driving it to the wall as it had with other British-owned car companies. In 1988, in desperation, the Thatcher government persuaded British Aerospace to buy the Rover Group, with the taxpayer writing off a huge debt. Then in 1994

John Major's Conservative government presided over the sale of Rover to the German car giant BMW. But by the year 2000 BMW was itself ready to abandon ship and sell the group. Chinese and Japanese car manufacturers hovered over the Rover Group as its fate was being decided. It was at this point that the TGWU, the largest of the unions affected by the decline of the Rover Group, moved onto the stage fighting for the existence of the company which by the year 2000 had reduced its Longbridge workforce to about 8,500. But of course the implications of Rover's crisis, allied to the general decline in the motor industry, concerned the entire Midlands region where thousands more workers in the car supply factories would be immediately affected. In effect the issue became focused on the future of all remaining British-owned car plants. This in essence was the challenge Bill Morris faced as leader of the major union involved. And it was on this barren crisis-ridden territory that he fought his last major battle both within and outside the union.

His principal opponent emerged from within the ranks of his own union, the national officer for the car industry, Tony Woodley. Yet this was far more complex and involved than a mere conflict between Bill Morris and Tony Woodley. It concerned the Blair government and especially the Chancellor, Gordon Brown; it included City of London finance houses hovering over the scene and looking for potentially lucrative pickings; it concerned foreign governments who, in Germany, China and Japan, all had interests in the future of Longbridge and Cowley and, above all, it brought the shadow of redundancy and unemployment over the heads of thousands of Midlands car workers who looked to their trade unions for protection. So how did this develop into a personal battle between Bill Morris and Tony Woodley? A battle that finally sealed the hostility that had long existed between the two men.

The timetable of decline and ultimate disaster is worth considering. In March 2000 BMW announced from its Munich headquarters that it was ready to sell off the Rover Group in Longbridge, though it wanted to keep the Mini production line at Oxford. It also revealed that it had started negotiations with an Anglo-German finance group called Alchemy whose senior partner, based in London, was Jon Moulton. The Alchemy plan was to reduce the Longbridge plant by about half the workforce and specialise in the production of the MG sports car. The name Rover would be replaced by a new title; MG Cars. Within ten days of this announcement mass demonstrations were organised by car workers in the Midlands, culminating in a rally of 80,000 in the centre of Birmingham on 1 April 2000. The rally was led by Tony Woodley of the TGWU who, with clear support, condemned the Alchemy deal as a 'complete sell-out' which threatened many thousands of jobs across the Midlands. Woodley's campaign was very effective. He knew that there was very little prospect of the government stepping in to save Longbridge. The then industry secretary in Blair's government, first Stephen Byers followed by his successor Patricia Hewitt, had made that clear. But the government wanted a deal to save jobs and the Chancellor, Gordon Brown, was actively involved in worldwide talks, including with the two state-run Chinese car groups, seeking to encourage them with tax incentives to invest in the Longbridge plant. A complex agenda made it very difficult for anyone to predict what would happen. But Tony Woodley was incensed by what he alleged was a Gordon Brown/ Bill Morris link in pursuing a deal with Alchemy. This is flatly denied by Morris. 'I never discussed Alchemy with Gordon Brown,' he insists. 'Any suggestion to the contrary is a blatant lie.' Tony Woodley himself refused to discuss the Alchemy proposal and even refused to take any phone calls from Jon Moulton. The only intervention by Morris was when he received a phone call from Moulton complaining about Woodley's refusal to even accept a telephone call. Woodley also rejected Morris's request that, at least, he should talk to Moulton.

In the meantime Woodley had started negotiations with a separate group, Phoenix Venture Holdings, which was Midlands-based and led by John Towers, a well-known local industrialist and a former Rover executive who had recruited a group of his old car industry managerial contacts. The outcome of all this frenetic activity was a deal in May 2000 when BMW sold the entire Longbridge plant to Phoenix for a token £10. In fact BMW paid Phoenix £500 million to take the group off its hands. BMW described that handout, with a sigh of relief, as a 're-structuring payment'. Technically that grant from BMW was supposed to be a loan to be repaid in three phases by 2049, but only if Rover made a profit. That sum was rapidly absorbed as Phoenix tried to rebuild the Rover Group after renaming it MG Rover and specialising in making MG cars. After five years the Phoenix venture collapsed with the management leaving under a cloud of bitter accusations, and Longbridge was bought out by two Chinese state-run car groups, Shanghai Automobile Industries Corporation and Nanjing Automobile Corporation. Most of the Longbridge workforce lost their jobs and the Midlands motor industry has never recovered. Indeed it was the first really dramatic closure in what has become a complete transformation in the old industrial culture of the Midlands. The entire British car industry had been virtually consumed by changing global economics, new technology and inferior management. The inquest into the Longbridge collapse has dragged on for years, and in July 2009 the British government announced yet another inquiry by the Serious Fraud Squad into the demise of MG Rover. The outcome remains uncertain – except that it has now been established by a government-commissioned report that the eventual collapse of MG Rover was indeed due to the mishandling and personal inadequacies of the so-called Phoenix Four.*

By the time MG Rover collapsed into the arms of the Chinese groups, Tony Woodley had become general secretary of the TGWU following Bill Morris's retirement in October 2003. Yet the debris from the extraordinary

---

* Government report, September 2009.

experiences when the fate of Longbridge was being resolved left an indelible mark across the already damaged relationship between Bill Morris and Tony Woodley. Without doubt Woodley had fought hard and with tenacious leadership to try to salvage something from the collapse of the Rover Group. Its ultimate failure was not his fault but down to the decline of the British car industry in general, left as it was to the mercy of its foreign competitors and dubious British management. Woodley's profile had been raised beyond his role as the union's national secretary for the motor industry, and in 2002 he was elected deputy general secretary when Margaret Prosser retired. Once again the union's second most senior position was filled by a firm critic of Bill Morris's leadership.* It was a poignant outcome when Morris had only one more year to serve as leader of the TGWU.

His final spell at the helm was very much a mixed cocktail of successes, disappointments, and some failures that often were beyond the control or reach of any trade union leader as the grievous Longbridge story demonstrated. Inevitably as he reflected over his decade as general secretary he was compelled to recognise the limitations as well as the privileges of his role at the top. He was repeatedly involved with the government over

---

* Prosser's predecessor was Jack Adams, former national secretary of the car-making section of the union. Adams was a leading communist figure in the union and persistent critic of Morris – ostensibly on political grounds but also known as an ally of Morris's critics on racial grounds and incompetent management.

race issues and often critical of the manner and the policies adopted by the Blair government which had been given another large overall majority in the general election of 2001. Morris was especially angry at the way some ministers handled, or failed to handle, the problems of rising immigration and particularly of asylum seekers. He campaigned against the government's moves to introduce a voucher system to provide social and financial relief to those immigrants who were genuine refugees from terror seeking asylum in Britain. He sustained a high-profile involvement in the inquiry into racial discrimination in the Metropolitan Police, notably after the horrific murder of young Stephen Lawrence and while serving with considerable effect on the Stephen Lawrence Task Group. The terms of reference for that committee were concerned with professional standards and workplace practices – not specifically with racial discrimination; but that, effectively, is what it amounted to.

In September 2001 Bill Morris presided over the 133rd Trades Union Congress at Brighton. It was, to be sure, a crowning honour and a Congress attended by Prime Minister Blair. He was then a mere two years away from retirement and in his presidential address opening the Congress he reflected back on his own extraordinary lifetime experience. Quietly and with solemn dignity he told the Congress: 'My journey from a small village in rural Jamaica to the Presidential Chair of this Congress has been a long and unexpected one. Many of my dreams along the way did not become realities. But it has been a journey where each reality was like a dream.'

9

The End Is a Beginning

IT WAS LATE ONE EVENING in the summer of 2009; the tea room in the Palace of Westminster was deserted. A declining sun sprawled shafts of long shadows across the largely empty room. The falling light made Lord Bill Morris of Handsworth look darker than he is, but he was unusually relaxed and at ease – a rare condition for him. He mostly manages to disguise his ease as well as unease exceptionally well. Detachment doesn't seem to worry him. Conversation had returned as it frequently did to his long battle with racial prejudice both inside, and to a lesser degree outside, his old trade union, the TGWU. Yet the issue had not before been confronted quite so directly, or as sharply as on that evening. He seemed ready to talk about it, with vigour and passion as well as derision of his critics. It was an unusual moment of candour. 'What did they want me to do? To learn how to do my job properly. Well I could and I did learn to do that. Or was it that they wanted me to be able to understand the British Labour Movement as well as they thought they understood it? Well I could read all about that – and I had. Or was it that they wanted me to change my colour from black to white? If that was it, then, no, I cannot do that, and wouldn't wish to.'

Perhaps this was Bill Morris's way of expressing the walled-up tensions that have emerged during the telling of his story. To be sure it is a story dominated by his endless battle against the overt and at times covert racial prejudice inside the TGWU, and of course such prejudice was far from confined to that or any other trade union. It has been, and still is, endemic across the breadth of all institutions, nor is it exclusive to Britain. Trevor Phillips, chairman of the Human Rights Commission is on record with this comment: 'If Barack Obama had lived here I would be very surprised if even somebody as brilliant as him would have been able to break through the institutional stranglehold ... on power within the Labour Party.'* That is a telling comment to offer as a backcloth to the story of Bill Morris's epic struggle; though the Morris story is proof that Mr Phillips can also misjudge the scene even if his Obama observation is not a strict analogy. That is because the Morris story is not simply a landmark as an account of one individual's fight for justice against the formidable prejudice Trevor Phillips was describing. More significantly it registered a historic turn in the political and social profile of the nation by reflecting the nature

---

* In November 2008 and re-quoted in the *Guardian*, 21 July 2009.

of cultural changes that have developed, sometimes unconsciously, and are still developing in Britain. Lord Bill became a one-man watershed in that process.

It is important to make these points at the outset of the chapter in which this story reaches its finale with the retirement of Bill Morris as general secretary of the TGWU. Moreover this is by no means the end of the Morris march against prejudice, nor of his impact and influence across British society as a whole. That continues not only in the House of Lords, but over a range of institutions, notably in various educational establishments including Chancellorship of the University of Staffordshire and his active association with London's South Bank University, the Open University, the University of Bedfordshire and the University of Northampton along with his continuing role as Chancellor at the University of Jamaica in Kingston. Sometimes he now resembles the perpetual motion of a visiting Professor of Experience as he travels the academic corridors. And then there is Lord Bill's rather special role as an influential member of the England and Wales Cricket Board. In fact he came close to occupying the chair of that most prestigious platform of the British Establishment. Nor is it an accident of gracious tokenism that he now holds the chairmanship of one of the EWCB's most important subcommittees, the one that determines the location of all Test Matches played in the UK and influences policy to provide amenities and facilities for spectators at the Test Match grounds. This is a role in which his experience as a trade union leader and a shrewd negotiator was seen as an inestimable advantage by the cricket establishment.

Of course Lord Bill's return to the cricket field is a clear throwback to his earliest roots and ambitions, when above all he aspired to play cricket for Jamaica and for the West Indies international test team. Now, as some consolation for missing that route, he has a privileged presence at Lord's cricket ground in London, the very home of the game he has never stopped loving. As a young boy at school in a small Jamaican farming village his overwhelming ambition was to become a professional cricketer and play for his country. In an interview with the *Sunday Telegraph** on the eve of presiding at that year's Trades Union Congress Morris was asked if he had his time over again and could choose between his role as a trade union leader and being a world class cricketer how would he respond. Without hesitation he replied: 'No choice at all – a world class cricketer playing for the West Indies. The hours are shorter and the grief is less.'

Instead chance, fate and the inner driving dream to rise from the remoteness of his birthplace led him eventually to become the leader of Britain's most powerful trade union, then also a cornerstone of the British Labour Party. In that sense he did become a form of British Obama an Obama of the British Labour Movement. That journey was an epic struggle between

---

* 10 September 2000.

Morris's willpower, his determined strength of character, and the prejudices he endured.

Yet there was an anticlimax to the story. The record of
Bill Morris's final moments of his tenure at the TGWU
still leave a bad taste in the mouth and a sense of guilt
in the mind of anyone who believes that the Labour
Movement is endowed, as always claimed, with the
socialist ethic. Those final stages of Bill Morris's role as
general secretary of the TGWU were filled with squalid
behaviour by those who succeeded him in October
2003. Tony Woodley was his successor as general secretary and after his election in the summer of 2003 Jack
Dromey, the main defeated candidate, was then elected
as deputy general secretary, Woodley's number two. By
that time the TGWU membership was already reduced
to about 800,000 and Woodley began by expediting a
merger with the large engineering union complex called
AMICUS that eventually merged into UNITE, now a
combination of nearly two million members. The character and the agenda of the old TGWU was changed
to meet the new social and industrial challenges that
were inevitably transforming the nature of trade unionism. Woodley and his closest colleagues at the top of the
union were convinced this was essential if the union was
to survive in a rapidly changing political and social climate. They had also long been persuaded that Bill Morris's agenda was misplaced and ill equipped to tackle
these problems. It is equally clear that personal conflicts
were frequently the determining element, even more so

than policy differences. In essence the Bill Morris/Tony Woodley relationship had soured at an early stage even before Woodley became a national officer: but the tension inevitably increased during Tony Woodley's highly effective years as the TGWU national officer for the motor industry. Details of their rupture during the fateful period when the future of the Rover car group was being decided have already been discussed. The finale was unusually unpleasant with the two men scarcely on speaking terms, and thus finding it impossible to have a normal working relationship. Morris departed in the autumn of 2003 without any formal retirement celebration. For the first time in the history of the TGWU a retiring general secretary departed without being given a farewell salute in the form of a substantial dinner accolade at a top London hotel. This could, and should, also have been an occasion to salute the knighthood which came to Morris in the Queen's birthday honours list in June 2003, shortly before his retirement. However Woodley made it clear that he was opposed to any such salute to his predecessor and made his views known across all regions of the union. Only one region, Region Five of the Midlands, Bill Morris's old base, defied what was in effect an edict from the new general secretary that there was to be no farewell salute to Morris. The secretary of Region Five, Gerard Coyne, ignored this and bravely organised a well-attended farewell dinner at the Birmingham Regency Hyatt Hotel on 24 January 2004. By then Bill Morris had been gone for nearly four months. The only member of the union's national hierarchy to attend the Birmingham function was Ray Collins, the man who had remained supportively alongside Bill Morris from his inception as general secretary.

Nor was this snub the last act in the tormenting twist to the Morris tale. By tradition the outgoing general secretary was allowed to keep his car as part of the retirement package. Morris asked for a replacement for his office car, a Jaguar, which he felt had run its course. Perhaps he was a touch over-demanding: a stand on a sense of entitlement. In any event Woodley was incensed by Morris's request for a new Jaguar and cancelled the car. Negotiations for a less expensive replacement were not completed for nearly a year after Morris's retirement. In fact the final stages of his departure from the Transport House headquarters in Theobalds Road, London, were dominated by an atmosphere of relentless if silent conflict. The outgoing general secretary invited a small and select group of his staff and supporters to a modest farewell drink in his office before he left. Since then he has not put a foot inside his old headquarters after his departure following his sixty-fifth birthday on 19 October 2003. Yet in one sense that was not the finale. This came unexpectedly following the death of Jack Jones on 21 April 2009. A carefully planned memorial service took place in honour of Jack Jones on 5 October 2009 at the Royal Festival Hall. Tony Woodley spent two to three months planning the occasion which was to be an event for the whole trade union and Labour Movement. A cast of star speakers were lined up – including Prime Minister Gordon Brown who had to cancel at the last moment. His place was taken by Lord Neil Kinnock, the former Labour leader. Woodley went to great lengths to ensure that the legendary Jack Jones was given a memorable send-off. A few days before the event Woodley made a personal phone call to Bill Morris inviting him to attend and, still more, to speak. Morris was taken completely by surprise – but he accepted Woodley's invitation as a significant gesture. He agreed to attend and was then personally introduced by Tony Woodley to a packed Festival Hall. The TGWU (now UNITE) general secretary spoke with genuine warmth about the union's honour in having the first black general secretary. It was a remarkable bid to heal old wounds. In response Bill Morris spoke with equal warmth about his old union.

On 11 April 2006 it was announced that Bill Morris would take a seat in the House of Lords as a working life peer and in June that year he was gazetted as Baron Morris of Handsworth in the county of West Midlands. This added to what had perhaps been an even more celebrated distinction when he was awarded the Order of Jamaica in 2002, a year before his retirement and his knighthood. Nowadays Lord Bill straddles the Atlantic as one of the Caribbean's most distinguished international figures as well as a unique man of Britain.

What of the scars? Bill Morris spends little time either contemplating them or even recognising their existence. But how much of a psychological denial is this? Of course he can and does now readily dismiss the prejudicial behaviour he experienced during his journey to the top of the TGWU. He can cast it aside with a casual wave of contempt. His social status is assured and confirmed; his record manifest. In one sense he is now part of the British Establishment – a label he would, for sure, dismiss with scorn. Yet there is truth within that paradox. His old uneasy lack of self-confidence has long since been overtaken by his achievements, his success and his acclaim. He is an altogether calmer, more relaxed person. Yet it is inevitable that some of the old scars remain, however well concealed and overshadowed by his contemporary distinction. In some respects his current temperament reminds one of the famed philosopher Isaiah Berlin who was always troubled, within himself, by the forms of ease his unease took – how could this only child of a Jewish timber merchant born in Riga in 1909 become so enamoured of his role at All Souls College, Oxford? The roots of our roots lie deeper than perhaps we are ready to recognise. And yet there is no doubt that the remarkable, if long-awaited, Festival Hall reconciliation move by Tony Woodley was quietly and warmly welcomed by Bill Morris. Perhaps he saw it as a vindicating climax; and perhaps it was.

'When I left the T&G I felt a sense of pride, not sadness,' Bill Morris insists. 'I left totally satisfied that I had done a good job for the union. I believe I had given back its self-respect and I had no complaints or worries. So I wasn't sad to go. I had come to the end of that journey and I knew I was closing an important chapter in my life and indeed in the union's life. Since then I have never been back. It's a closed chapter. I certainly wasn't going to allow the reactionary bigots inside the T&G to wreck my life.'

Did he have any regrets? He admits to a few. 'I think I was probably too cautious about mergers. I wanted to organise a merger with the GMB union* rather than with the engineering union AMICUS but that didn't come off. I would also have liked to arrange a link-up with the building workers union UCATT. I certainly should have gone for that merger with more energy. It was a bad decision not to have done so. But I didn't want mergers simply for the sake of having more members. My aim was to help the T&G and the trade union movement in general ... but there it is ...' He waved a hand at history and to what might have been.

Bill Morris confesses to one other important regret: a failure to pay sufficient attention to his succession. As his retirement approached he did consider the then Scottish region secretary Jimmy Elsby as a potential successor but dropped the idea. He then hesitated over Jack Dromey – a one-time close ally who later turned opponent and contested him during the bitter and politically (and racially) dramatic second-term election for general secretary. Despite this, Morris regarded Dromey as

---

* GMB is the acronym for the General, Municipal and Boilermakers' union, an amalgamation of several general unions and the craft union, the Boilermakers' Society.

a likely successor given his record in the union – notably his fifteen years as national secretary for the public services group. But the final period of internal tension at the top undermined his possible support and regard for Dromey. In the end it was Woodley's forceful leadership as national secretary for the motor industry that propelled him through as the most popular candidate for succession – made all the more likely when Woodley was elected deputy general secretary on the retirement of Margaret Prosser. That was, to be sure, a victory resented by Bill Morris. But it settled the issue. Tony Woodley was now in charge and Dromey was subsequently elected as Woodley's deputy. Morris's instinctive resentment at that combination was predictable and understandable. As Morris turned away from the union, despite his ostensible stoicism, the scars were visible.

Ray Collins, who is now general secretary of the Labour Party, has no doubt about the crucial importance of Bill Morris's period as leader of the TGWU. His succinct overall verdict on Morris is: 'He saved the union.' Collins is convinced that it was Bill Morris's determined drive to re-organise the union that helped rescue the TGWU from a serious crisis. He points to the crucial changes made by Morris: cutting down the number of regional offices, making significant economies where in some areas there had been manifest overspending, and modernising the union's structure. Collins also attributes much of this to the advice and strategy that

Peter Regnier brought to the union. But he emphasises that it was Morris's determination, his courage and refusal to be deterred by the prejudices surrounding him that combined to help rebuild and save the union. 'In fact he was a better manager than Ron Todd,' Collins claims. 'It is not true that we ever faced bankruptcy as some people have claimed but there was a very serious financial situation.' What most of all outraged and disgusted Collins was the racial prejudice against Morris. 'The plotting was endemic, as was the racism,' he adds, 'I was frankly disgusted by the anti-Bill Morris racism right across the political spectrum – the Left often more so than the Right.' But Collins is not without his own criticism of his former chief. 'He wasn't an easy person to deal with. Sometimes he would simply cut himself off from the world and go into a kind of purdah. He was always a very private person and sometimes found it difficult to relate even with his closest colleagues.' Yet Collins also recognises that when the shutters came down it was often because a defensive mechanism took over. 'How can we know,' he mused, 'it isn't possible unless you can transmute yourself and realise how it feels to be black in such a situation facing those experiences.'

Such criticism of Bill Morris's difficulties in relating to those around him was commonplace across the union – among friends and allies as well as critics and opponents. Even some of his closest friends and supporters on the TUC General Council – men like Rodney Bickerstaffe – could never quite understand why Bill Morris always refused to become more closely associated with the moderate left group on the TUC which Bickerstaffe led: 'Cautious, defensive, private and keeping himself to himself. It didn't affect my affection and support for him but I never quite felt I could actually get behind his defensive wall.'

So what does lie behind the private image of Bill Morris? What has shaped the man who is now Lord Bill Morris of Handsworth? What lies beneath the surface of his public persona?

In many ways Bill Morris has never cast off the mantle of his earliest childhood influences. They were first formed in his birthplace village of Bombay in the hinterland of Jamaica, sixty miles from the capital of Kingston. It was there and in the nearby still smaller village of Mizpah where the young Morris was brought into the local Baptist Church community in which his mother, Una, and his maternal grandmother were active congregants. The Church was a factor in his early development with its strong moral and ethical code focused on community help, social discipline and unflinching assistance to the less fortunate. It was that cradle of experience which left a deep impact on the mind of young Bill Morris and doubtless shaped the man who was to become Britain's first black trade union leader. It was a mission to help those in need.

Of course as most psychologists – notably Freud – maintain, it is our childhood experiences which form the essential base on which all subsequent emotional impulses and characteristics are established. Bill Morris never understates his deep and endemic attachment to his roots. Consciously and still more subconsciously, his adult years in Britain and especially his experiences as leader of the Transport Union reflect this background. Even his early boyhood shyness comes through as a foretaste of the subsequent enclosed persona. Previous chapters show how he developed a kind of protective armour against the racial prejudices that surrounded his promotion up the ladder before he finally became general secretary of the TGWU – and once he occupied that top role the self-protective shield became still more evident. Bill Morris essentially is a deeply private person. Yet even that basic truism hides a reality. There are two fundamental elements to his character: first and most visible is an outward charm of friendliness with a quick smile and matching gestures; yet this conceals a firmly protected inner man whose deeper levels of feeling are rarely revealed to the outside world or even his friends. The gregariousness one would assume to be a routine condition among all trade union leaders never came easily to Bill Morris. Even those close to him – a small minority – inside the union as well as across the wider Labour Movement often found and still find an enclosed man difficult to penetrate; a man seeming to hold something in reserve or, as described by his friend Rodney Bickerstaffe: 'Bill always seemed to play off the back foot' – an analogy which fits well for a man who always wanted to be a professional cricketer rather than a trade union leader. Bickerstaffe is by no means alone with this essentially friendly observation. Several other trade union leaders have agreed: 'Bill always preferred to remain his own man – very much a loner, perhaps seeking to prove to himself as well as to others that he was not dependent on closer friendships.'

Some also noted Bill Morris's smart style of clothing with some surprise. He would almost always turn up carefully dressed, only rarely appearing in casual clothing. Inside the TGWU various critics would choose to regard his style of dress as 'showmanship' – and perhaps make the snide and snickering remarks that all this suited a member of the Bank of England Court and, later, a member of the House of Lords. If Morris was ever aware of such facile criticism he never responded to it – nor did it influence his habit. Perhaps subconsciously it might have registered in his mind as yet another manifestation of racial prejudice – i.e. black men seeking to match the elegant attire of 'posh' white men. In any event his private emotions are kept permanently under control and the Morris guard is rarely relaxed. The one exception visible to most who knew him at the time was when his wife Minetta died in January 1990. He described that loss as 'irreparable'. That well-known quiet dignity of Bill Morris, his protective armour against an outside world that sometimes seemed hostile, was momentarily penetrated. It was an unusually visible sign of a profoundly emotional man beneath an outward carapace of calmness. It was also a moment when he did feel very much a lone figure without Minetta by his side and when a touch of understandable insecurity hovered over him.

Bill Morris was fifty-one when Minetta died – two years before he took over as general secretary of the TGWU on the retirement of his predecessor Ron Todd. Those who worked closely with him through the turbulent years of his leadership believe Morris became increasingly self-enclosed after Minetta's death – though at the same time demonstrating even greater courage and determination when under attack from his detractors within his own union. Ray Collins, his closest ally and supporter within the TGWU hierarchy, was ever impressed by Morris's capacity to deal with his critics without outward manifestations of rancour. His courage was only rarely on public display; there were no theatrics, only the quiet determination to do his job to the best of his capacity and prove his opponents wrong. It was as if he was consciously fighting any sense of insecurity with a determined will to be tougher, stronger and more single-minded than ever. In that sense he clearly found his privacy shield an additional protection.

Even his work for various charities was kept under wraps. The TUC general secretaries with whom Morris worked closely, John Monks and Brendan Barber, both refer to Morris's work for various charities and his insistence on keeping the information strictly private. Both TUC leaders saw this as characteristic of Morris's style. Just as he has always maintained a discreet silence over frequent visits to various black community centres where, as he quietly describes: 'I go to meet people to talk about things that really matter.' Now, where possible, he prefers the quiet life away from the political ambience of Westminster. He and his partner Eileen have a London flat but whenever practical spend time in their main home in Shropshire where they occupy themselves walking, reading and listening to jazz – his favoured music.

Bill Morris's two sons Clyde and Garry are close to their father but have had no link with his working life. They were rarely seen in his company when he was a trade union leader nor do they have any open connection with their father's political life as an active Labour peer in the House of Lords. And apart from references to his role as a proud grandfather Bill Morris does not talk about family matters. Like all else in his private life such discussion remains sealed away.

None of this suggests that Bill Morris rejoices in any hermit-like lifestyle. Far from it. He enjoys the company of friends who vary from a small inner circle to a broader sweep which includes old contacts from the political community, but more recently new friends in both the cricketing establishment as well as the House of Lords.

Bill Morris's relationship with his original mentor, George Wright, is another revealing element – notably in Wright's own assessment of the man who defeated him for the general secretary role. Wright remained a critical admirer and certainly an honourable opponent who despised those in the union who used racial motives to spur their criticism of the general secretary. George Wright consistently refused to join the racial claque.

All of them – admirers, critics, supporters, opponents – share the Ray Collins assessment of a remarkable man who was never really easy to know. What is
Bill Morris's reaction to this; a shrug, of course but also
a further revealing afterthought on his role: 'I was the
right man at the right time for the union.' He reminds
us all that he became general secretary of the TGWU at
a moment when the entire social, political and certainly
the cultural scene in Britain was in flux; when everything, not just the role and functions of trade unionism,
was changing. Margaret Thatcher's legacy handed onto
John Major was the political condition of Britain; it was
pre-Blair and then it became Blair's Britain with all the
disappointment that period brought to people like Bill
Morris. Such was the epoch of change which straddled
Morris's leadership of the TGWU.

The curtain has fallen on that period and that extraordinary experience. In this context it is worth record-
ing Lord Bill's continuing private links with his original
roots in Britain – Handsworth in Birmingham. He
returns there frequently for quiet moments with various relatives and friends. He has two aunts in the area
whom he visits from time to time. He even goes back
to his old firm Hardy Spicer and recently took part in a
BBC programme about his early days in Birmingham.
His mother is buried in a cemetery in Handsworth
where he pays regular visits to her grave. Perhaps most
revealing of all he still goes back to his old barber in
Handsworth for a haircut. Roots mean a great deal to

him; in England as well as in Jamaica. But home as such is where he is. It is also his prime protection. He admits to be being 'a home lover'. For Lord Bill home is where he feels safest. 'I like being at home. It's a great relaxation for me. I can be me. I can sit on the carpet and eat my beans on toast. Home is like a citadel where I am very safe, very protected.' He reads a lot and his partner Eileen – they have been together for about seventeen years – helps to choose his books. He keeps in touch with his sons and two grandchildren. But he guards his private life with great care.

He likes to escape from London to the home in the countryside he shares with Eileen, and the precise identity of which he prefers to keep private. Far away from the House of Lords and even further away from his trade union background: though not too far from a cricket pitch. 'Frankly,' he confesses, 'life has never been better.'

One gets the feeling that Lord Bill has arrived at his preferred wicket.

Biographical Notes

19 OCTOBER 1938	Born Bombay, Jamaica.
NOVEMBER 1954	Arrival in United Kingdom.
1956	Joined Transport and General Workers Union.
1956	Married to Minetta Smith.
NOVEMBER 1957	Birth of first son: Clyde Arthur Morris.
NOVEMBER 1958	Birth of second son: Garry Alexander Morris.
1962	Elected shop steward at Hardy Spicer, Birmingham.
1971	Elected to TGWU General Executive Council.
1973	Appointed a full-time official of the TGWU; as district organiser in the Nottingham office of the union.
1976	Promoted to district secretary at Northampton office of the TGWU.
17 SEPTEMBER 1985	Appointed deputy general secretary; number two to general secretary Ron Todd.

JANUARY 1990	Death of wife Minetta.
7 JUNE 1991	Elected general secretary, to take up office in 1992.
1991/92	Meets Eileen Ware, a social worker in London working with the board of Project Fullemploy – a training organisation for young people. She becomes Morris's partner.
1992	Takes over from Ron Todd as general secretary in March 1992.
1994	Sale of Transport House, traditional home of the TGWU.
1995	Move to Palace Court headquarters near Victoria in January 1995.
1995	Re-elected general secretary after the national ballot amid great bitterness.
1998	Appointed to the Court of the Bank of England.
1999	Appointed first Chancellor of the University of Technology. Kingston, Jamaica.
1999	Appointed member of the Royal Commission on Reform of the House of Lords.
SEPTEMBER 2001	President of the Trades Union Congress.
JUNE 2003	Awarded a knighthood on the Queen's birthday honours list, becoming Sir Bill Morris prior to his retirement.

19 OCTOBER 2003	Retired as general secretary of the TGWU on his 65th birthday.
2004	Appointed Chancellor of Staffordshire University.
11 APRIL 2006	It was announced that Sir Bill Morris would take a seat in the House of Lords as Baron Morris of Handsworth in the county of the West Midlands.

Bibliography

Allen V. L. *Trade Union Leadership*. London, Longmans, 1957

Bullock Lord Ala. *The Life and Times of Ernest Bevin* London, Heinemann, Vo1.1 [1960] Vo1.2 [1967]

Brendon, Piers. *The Decline and Fall of the British Empire 1781–1997*: London, Jonathan Cape, 2007

Coates, Ken & Topham, Tony. *The Making of the Transport and General Workers Union. Volume 1 [two parts]*. Oxford, Blackwell, 1991

Gilmour, Lord Ian. *Dancing with Dogma; Britain under Thatcherism;* London, Simon & Schuster, 1992

Goodman, Geoffrey. *The Awkward Warrior; Frank Cousins; His Life and Times.* London, Davis-Poynter, 1979; Nottingham, Spokesman Books, 1984

Jones, Jack. *Union Man – an Autobiography.* London, Collins, 1986

Kavanagh, Dennis. *Thatcherism and British Politics;* Oxford, Oxford University Press, 1990

Murray, Andrew. *The T&G Story; A History of the Transport And General Workers Union, 1922–2007,* London, Lawrence & Wishart and UNITE, 2008

Riddell, Peter. *The Thatcher Government.* Oxford, Martin, Robinson, 1983

TGWU. *Official minutes of the General Executive Council of the TGWU; and sub-committees,* London, UNITE [TGWU section], 1979–2003. [note; limited access]

TUC. *Annual Reports of Trades Union Congress;* Circa, 1985- 2003. London, TUC

Williams, Francis. *Magnificent Journey;* London, Odhams Press, 1954

Acknowledgements

THE LATE PROFESSOR SIR BERNARD CRICK in his introduction to a famed biography of George Orwell wrote: 'The labour of writing a biography, like the education of a child, involves a prolonged and strange mixture of love and critical distance, of commitment and restraint.' I know of no biographer who has summed up the problem with greater clarity. It is a prolonged wrestle between various levels of judgement: the pursuit of information, a constant awareness of the traps laid by that all-seducing temptress called 'Truth' and the perpetual reminder that in writing about any individual it is imperative to appreciate that the subject, like the rest of us, has several different layers of character each jostling for supremacy, for presentation as the public image. Perhaps, as Chesterton observed, that is why many of the best biographies are quasi-novels.

However this is not a novel. It is, I trust, a reasonably balanced factual portrait of a remarkable man. What is indisputable is that this book could not have been attempted and certainly not completed without the

enormous help I have received from many friends, especially those in the old Transport and General Workers
Union and in this respect most of all from the subject
himself, Bill Morris. He was a reluctant starter. He was
never enamoured of the project. His natural shyness
and cultivated privacy offered hurdles. But he relented
and agreed to co-operate – without which I would not
have agreed to write it. To him I owe the biggest debt of
thanks – though it needs to be emphasised that this is
not an authorised biography in the strict sense.

But I cannot exclude from my list those friends
inside the TGWU whose help, advice and guidance
have been absolutely invaluable. The list is substantial
but I must begin with my thanks to Ray Collins, the
former assistant general secretary of the union who is
now general secretary of the Labour Party; his help and
support have been outstanding. I owe a similar debt of
gratitude to George Wright, now retired from his role
as the union's regional secretary for Wales, and to Brian
Mathers, the retired former regional secretary of the
T&G in the Midlands. To my roll of thanks I wish to
add Andrew Murray and his staff at the union, notably Irene Dykes and Lorraine Diales; to Brian Revell,
a retired national secretary of the union and to many
others in that very special trade union which now goes
under its newly branded label of UNITE. A number of
them wished to remain anonymous since their information could compromise their continuing employment as officials of UNITE.

I wish also to add my grateful thanks to Brendan

Barber, general secretary of the TUC and to his predecessor John Monks who is now general secretary of the European TUC; to Rodney Bickerstaffe, the former general secretary of UNISON, to Lord David Lea, a former assistant general secretary at the TUC; to the chief archivist and his team at the Records Department of Warwick University and to the TUC library, along with numerous other friends and contacts including a number of senior Labour Party political figures who prefer to remain anonymous but whose help has been equally invaluable. I would also wish to add Eileen Ware, Bill Morris's partner, to my list of appreciation. She preferred to remain in the background though her support and encouragement was nonetheless crucial to the whole process.

At the end of the day, of course, as is customary I must emphasise that the contents and views contained in the book are entirely my responsibility. The errors, where they occur, are my own. No one but the author can stand blamed for such blemishes.

My final, though by no means least, encomium of gratitude goes to my wife Margit and my family for having to put up with the eccentricities, foibles and often hardship of having an ageing husband, father, grandfather and indeed great-grandfather spending so much time in monastic authorship. I am indebted to them all for their loving support.

Geoffrey Goodman
October 2009